Praise for *VISIBLE LEARNING*

As I read this book I became increasingly aware of my own self-talk saying, "yes, of course, that's absolutely right, that's what we must do, now I get it." The authors reassert a vital humanist approach to what, how and why students learn about their societies, history, culture and the wider world around them. It reminds us that we have a duty to prepare young minds for complex global challenges with a deep, critical, and nuanced understanding.

> —Neville Kirton, Deputy Head of Secondary (9–11),
> Colegio Anglo Colombiano, International Baccalaureate

Having a resource like this—with so many applicable strategies and examples—will assert a conversation around social studies education in my division. This resource aligns with our division's goal of more rigorous and relevant assessment, paired with appropriate feedback.

> —Vince Bustamante, Social Studies Curriculum Consultant

VISIBLE LEARNING® for Social Studies is an instructional treasure trove for teachers of social studies. The authors offer practical, usable, and specific instructional strategies that work best at the surface, deep, and transfer phases of learning with examples from kindergarten to grade 12. In today's world of mass media, social studies lessons must engage students in learning at deeper levels and help them develop a fluency in critical literacy skills. With that purpose, this book is a must-have, must-use text for all social studies teachers.

> —Cathy J. Lassiter, EdD, Former High School Social Studies Department Chair
> and Senior Director of Instruction in Norfolk, VA

This book is a wonderful addition to any busy teacher or curriculum writer's library. Meant for K–12, it is easy to read and implementable at any point in the year. The strategies provided teach students to utilize their background knowledge but dare to think critically in unfamiliar situations.

> —Heather Giustiniani, International Baccalaureate
> Primary Years Programme Coordinator

As a nationwide movement grows to provide greater support for K–12 social studies education, books like this provide first-hand, data-driven recommendations for how educators can enhance student learning in this space. If you are part of the effort to improve social studies education in this country, you should read this book.

> —Julie Silverbrook, Executive Director,
> The Constitutional Sources Project (www.ConSource.org)

VISIBLE LEARNING® *for Social Studies* will inspire teachers, guide curriculum coordinators and instructional coaches, and will help educators bring transfer and thinking back into the humanities classroom. This book will help humanities teaches rediscover the value of their subject and will revitalize their approach to designing learning.

—J. Rafael Ángel, Concept-Based Curriculum and Instruction Trainer
and Consultant; MYP Coordinator, GIS Dubai

This is that unicorn of education books; it combines compelling classroom stories with accessible, relevant information about the research undergirding the change ideas. It is rich with resources and tools that teachers can use to make immediate changes in their units, but more than that, it will inspire teachers to pursue their own change ideas and research as they work to create just and equitable classroom communities.

—Angela Wilcox, IB MYP Coordinator, Hopkins Public Schools, MN

This book is a game-changer! I am so excited to have a Visible Learning book that speaks specifically to the daily challenges of social studies teachers! It has become clear that social studies education is vital to the health of democracy, but there seem to be many divergent views on what high-quality social studies education looks like. Based on high-quality evidence, the authors point us to a few key strategies that are especially important in the social studies classroom.

Instead of arguing endlessly about content versus skills, teachers now have an evidence-based guidebook to help understand which learning strategies are most effective at a specific phase in the learning. Why do my classroom discussions fall flat? Why did my historical simulation fall apart? How can I make my vocabulary activities relevant and engaging? This book can help be a guide for teachers at all stages of their careers to help understand when different learning strategies are going to be most successful!

Use this as a base text to springboard collaborative learning with colleagues in social studies. The book includes so many strategies that we can explore together to become real agents of learning and change.

VISIBLE LEARNING® *for Social Studies* targets disciplinary literacy and explains the common pitfalls. The authors include so many good tips, like modeling our disciplinary thinking, and describe the most common mistakes, like focusing only on surface knowledge or asking students deep or transfer questions when they haven't acquired the basic content.

I was delighted to find that the authors used international content and vignettes. The examples and inclusive language reflect our Canadian provincial standards, outcomes, and expectations.

—Rachel Collishaw, President, Ontario History and Social Science Teachers'
Association (OHASSTA) and Social Studies Educators' Network of Canada (SSENC)

While most books on educational pedagogy focus on areas outside of social studies, *VISIBLE LEARNING®* *for Social Studies* takes John Hattie's critical work and makes it accessible for social studies teachers. The authors provide a clear and practical guide to implementing the most effective, evidence-based teaching strategies that will engage your social studies students. This book is a must-read for social studies teachers of all grade levels.

—Kevin Lopuck, President—Mantinoba Social Science Teachers' Association (MSSTA), Department Head—Social Studies, Lord Selkirk Regional Comprehensive Secondary School, Selkirk, MB, Canada

All teachers need access to research-based, high impact strategies, shared in a way that we can easily see how to put them to use directly in our classrooms. This book puts together the research-basis and the practical strategies in a way that will help teachers hit the ground running in increasing the impact of the work we do to help our students learn.

—Catherine McCall, Social Studies Education, University of Maryland

This book is a treasure trove of instructional strategies illustrated through compelling classroom vignettes and accompanied by the theories and research that enriched my understanding of how learning happens. With each chapter I felt both challenged and empowered to teach better. How rare it is to find a book so informative and inspiring!

—Krista Ferraro, History Department Chair, Thayer Academy

VISIBLE LEARNING® for Social Studies is a wonderful and needed addition to the VISIBLE LEARNING® series. Julie Stern's Conceptual Understanding work enhances our understanding of how social studies learning could engage students in connecting big ideas in humanities to thinking about twentieth century challenges.

—Ainsley B. Rose, Corwin Author Consultant

A call for all social studies teachers, the book you have been waiting for has arrived. VISIBLE LEARNING® for Social Studies packages the most compelling research in education and some essential social science content knowledge into one book. The book is written in a way that a busy social studies teacher could pick it up, flip to the section relevant to their situation, and find answers that can be translated into their classroom immediately.

—Teresa Rensch, Director of Curriculum and Instruction
Konocti Unified School District
Lower Lake, CA

Hattie, Fisher, Frey, and Stern have provided a laser-like focus for social studies teachers. This book masterfully integrates *why* developing certain skills is critical to growing in an understanding of concepts with *how* to practically design an impactful curriculum to guide social studies students toward transfer of both. The authors expertly match specific strategies with the optimal time in learning to use them for the greatest impact and provide the perfect blend of "why," "what," and "how." No stone is left unturned. Any social studies teacher that embraces VISIBLE LEARNING®

for Social Studies, novice or veteran, will quickly move from surface to transfer in their own skills and subsequently accelerate their students' growth and love of the content. What teacher doesn't want that?

—Steve Oertle, Assistant Superintendent
Roxana Community Unit School District #1
Roxana, IL

This is definitely a "just right" read for educators who want to deepen their knowledge about VISIBLE LEARNING® research, identify high-impact practices that influence student learning, and develop their ability to know which high-impact practices to implement at just the right time of their students' learning phase—surface, deep, or transfer. With clear examples, strategies and tools, *VISIBLE LEARNING® for Social Studies* is a practical resource for educators who are ready for the challenge of improving their own practice and empowering students to own their learning.

—Meg Roa, Professional Learning Specialist
Volusia County Schools
Volusia, FL

At a time when conceptual understanding in social studies has been somewhat neglected, *VISIBLE LEARNING® for Social Studies, Grades K–12* reminds teachers about the importance of surface level, deep, and transferable understandings of important social studies concepts. Further, the authors provide tools for teachers to build such conceptual understanding, along with disciplinary skills, at a time when both are vital to democratic societies.

—Jeffery D. Nokes, Associate Professor, History
Brigham Young University

The next content area impacted by the Visible Learning research has been released at an important time for teaching and learning in social studies. The authors have done a fine job connecting the research in the context of the social studies classroom. Most importantly, the authors spend an entire chapter guiding the teacher in the process of moving social studies from an area of static facts and repeated themes through history, to a depth of learning calling for students to synthesize and apply their learning at deeper levels.

VISIBLE LEARNING® for Social Studies guides the classroom teacher to create assessment capable learners in the context of the social studies curriculum at a time when citizenry benefits from deep learning in the social sciences!

—Dr. Terry Mootz, EdD
Associate Superintendent
J Sterling Morton HS District 201
Cicero, IL

VISIBLE LEARNING®
for Social Studies
Grades K–12

VISIBLE LEARNING®
for Social Studies
Grades K–12

Designing Student Learning for
Conceptual Understanding

John Hattie

Julie Stern

Douglas Fisher

Nancy Frey

CORWIN

FOR INFORMATION:

Corwin
A SAGE Company
2455 Teller Road
Thousand Oaks, California 91320
(800) 233-9936
www.corwin.com

SAGE Publications Ltd.
1 Oliver's Yard
55 City Road
London EC1Y 1SP
United Kingdom

SAGE Publications India Pvt. Ltd.
B 1/I 1 Mohan Cooperative Industrial Area
Mathura Road, New Delhi 110 044
India

SAGE Publications Asia-Pacific Pte. Ltd.
18 Cross Street #10-10/11/12
China Square Central
Singapore 048423

Acquisitions Editor: Ariel Curry
Associate Content
  Development Editor: Jessica Vidal
Associate Editor: Eliza Erickson
Production Editor: Rebecca Lee
Copy Editor: Tammy Giesmann
Typesetter: C&M Digitals (P) Ltd.
Proofreader: Rae-Ann Goodwin
Indexer: Integra
Cover Designer: Rose Storey
Marketing Manager: Deena Meyer

Printed in the United States of America.

Library of Congress Control Number (LCCN) 2020002763

ISBN 978-1-5443-8082-7

This book is printed on acid-free paper.

SUSTAINABLE FORESTRY INITIATIVE
Certified Chain of Custody
At Least 10% Certified Forest Content
www.sfiprogram.org
SFI-01028

24 25 26 27 12 11 10 9 8 7

Contents

Visit the companion website at
http://resources.corwin.com/VL-socialstudies
for downloadable resources.

List of Figures

List of Videos

Note from the Publisher: The authors have provided video and web content throughout the book that is available to you through QR (quick response) codes. To read a QR code, you must have a smartphone or tablet with a camera. We recommend that you download a QR code reader app that is made specifically for your phone or tablet brand.

Videos may also be accessed at
http://resources.corwin.com/VL-socialstudies

About the Authors

Professor John Hattie is an award-winning education researcher and best-selling author with nearly 30 years of experience examining what works best in student learning and achievement. His research, better known as Visible Learning®, is a culmination of nearly 30 years synthesizing more than 1,500 meta-analyses comprising more than 90,000 studies involving over 300 million students around the world. He has presented and keynoted in over 350 international conferences and has received numerous recognitions for his contributions to education. His notable publications include *Visible Learning*, *Visible Learning for Teachers*, *Visible Learning and the Science of How We Learn*, *Visible Learning for Mathematics, Grades K–12*, and, most recently, *10 Mindframes for Visible Learning*. Learn more about his research at www.corwin.com/visiblelearning.

Julie Stern is the best-selling author of *Tools for Teaching Conceptual Understanding, and Elementary and Secondary*, which are Visible Learning Supporting Resources. She is the thought leader behind the global workshop series, Making Sense of Learning Transfer, and is a certified trainer in Visible Learning Plus. Her passion is synthesizing the best of education research into practical tools that support educators in breaking free of the industrial model of schooling and moving toward teaching and learning that promotes sustainability, equity, and well-being. She is a James Madison Constitutional Fellow and taught social studies for many years in Washington, DC and her native Louisiana. Julie moves internationally every few years with her husband, a US diplomat, and her two young sons. Her website is www.edtosavetheworld.com.

Douglas Fisher, PhD, is Professor of Educational Leadership at San Diego State University and a leader at Health Sciences High and Middle College. He has served as a teacher, language development specialist, and administrator in public schools and non-profit organizations, including eight years as Director of Professional Development for the City Heights Collaborative, a time of increased student achievement in some of San Diego's urban schools. Doug has engaged in professional learning communities for several decades, building teams that design and implement systems to impact teaching and learning. He has published numerous books on teaching and learning, such as *Assessment-Capable Visible Learners* and *Engagement by Design*.

Nancy Frey, PhD, is a Professor in Educational Leadership at San Diego State University and a leader at Health Sciences High and Middle College. She has been a special education teacher, reading specialist, and administrator in public schools. Nancy has engaged in professional learning communities as a member and in designing schoolwide systems to improve teaching and learning for all students. She has published numerous books, including *The Teacher Clarity Playbook* and *Rigorous Reading*.

Acknowledgments

Corwin gratefully acknowledges the contributions of the following reviewers:

Vince Bustamante, Social Studies Curriculum Consultant
Edmonton Catholic Schools
Edmonton, AB Canada

Rick Gilson, Executive Director
Southern Alberta Professional Development Consortium
Magrath, AB, Canada

Meg Roa, District Administrator; Professional Learning Specialist
Volusia County Schools
DeLand, FL

Kim Sergent, Middle/High Social Studies teacher
Kentucky Valley Educational Cooperative
Hazard, KY

LAYING THE GROUNDWORK FOR VISIBLE LEARNING® FOR SOCIAL STUDIES

1

What does the future hold when the vast majority of middle and high school students are unable to tell the difference between an online news story and an advertisement (Wineburg, 2019)? Or when they fail to answer basic questions about slavery in the United States or about the Holocaust (Shuster, 2018)? Or when 24 percent of US millennials considered democracy to be a *bad* or *very bad* way of running the country (Levine & Kawashima-Ginsberg, 2017, p. 3)? Healthy, thriving democracies depend upon an educated citizenry. Today's social studies teachers face new challenges that have significant consequences.

Picture a middle school classroom where students begin their geography lesson by viewing images of an oil rig, a boat full of freshly caught fish, a pile of raw cut emeralds, a large freshwater lake, and a field of wind turbines. The students discuss what these images have in common and determine that they are all *things we use from the earth*. Their teacher, Katie Robinson, clarifies that these are examples of the concept called *natural resources*. She then defines *natural resources* and asks students to complete an elaboration activity to make meaning of the term for themselves. The next day, she provides several choices of articles to read about various natural resources so that students can see the application of this term. The students complete a short journal prompt to summarize their understanding of the term *natural resources*.

What did you notice about these instructional strategies? Ms. Robinson does not jump straight to asking students to evaluate a country's access to natural resources until she is sure that her students understand what the term *natural resources* means, helping them to identify the critical attributes as exemplified across multiple examples. This is surface level learning done well, which we will focus on in Chapter 2. Surface level learning is when students explore new concepts and build initial understanding. The next day, students conduct similar activities with the concepts of *scarcity* and *power*. Ms. Robinson explains that they are going to look at situations in which there is a limited supply of natural resources and that, eventually, they will extrapolate the relationship that scarcity, natural resources, and power have in each situation. When students make generalizations about the relationships between and among concepts, they are moving into the deep learning phase, which we will explore in Chapter 3.

Next, Ms. Robinson models how she analyzes primary and secondary source documents using a strategy called IREAD (Monte-Sano, Paz, & Felton, 2014), which we will describe in Chapter 2. The students practice annotating a primary source document in small groups while Ms. Robinson circulates to check their conversations and offer feedback on their work. In this case, the students are back at surface level learning for source analysis, even though they are simultaneously in deeper levels of learning as they examine the relationships among scarcity, natural resources, and power. Next, she introduces the scenario of the Nile River and students complete a jigsaw activity with both primary and secondary sources to find out more information about the water crisis on the Nile. While completing graphic organizers, students begin to notice that there is relative power among nations such as South Sudan, with proportionally little international power compared to Egypt. They begin to grasp the role that international power plays in situations where natural resources are scarce. Deep learning occurs when students start to generalize to broader rules about how concepts interact, and we will examine this phase in more detail in Chapter 3.

Ms. Robinson's students are now ready to transfer their learning to a new situation where natural resources, scarcity, and power play a role. We will investigate the transfer phase of learning more carefully in Chapter 4.

The point here is to see that Ms. Robinson is intentional about the phase of learning her students are in and plans accordingly. **Surface level learning** occurs when students gain initial understanding of the concepts, terms, skills, facts, and vocabulary of a topic. **Deep learning** occurs when students begin to make connections between these ideas and generalize about broader principles based on their classroom experiences. **Transfer of learning** occurs when students apply these connections to new situations. The other key aspect is that students increase their independence from one phase to the next and begin to choose among their understanding and skills to suit the new situation at hand. See Figure 1.1 for a chart of the instructional strategies shown in each phase of the example above. The remaining chapters of this book will provide details about each of these phases and instructional strategies.

With limited instructional time and numerous standards or learning outcomes to teach, the question for social studies teachers is: How do we maximize precious time to ensure that students grasp enough to prepare them for informed civic life? The discipline of social studies is far more than memorizing dates and facts. It involves the skillful ability to conduct investigations, analyze sources, place events in historical and cultural context, and synthesize various points of view, while recognizing our own biases. Recent developments in the field ask us to reorient our thinking about good social studies instruction—moving from one of passive memorization of facts and dates to a more dynamic process of disciplinary inquiry. We need to teach students how to evaluate and synthesize vast amounts of information, analyze divergent points of view, and work collaboratively to build prosperous and fair societies.

Doug remembers his US history class. We created pages and pages of outlines from the history textbook. We used the headings from the textbook as the major organizer and included details under each heading. We were required to include each bold word in our notes. On Fridays, we watched a movie that was somehow related to the chapter and took more notes. Some of the movies were documentary and some were tangentially related stories. On Mondays, we took a test on the information from the week before. And then the process started anew. The teacher never talked in class, other than when students misbehaved.

EXAMPLE OF SURFACE, DEEP, AND TRANSFER STRATEGIES IN GEOGRAPHY

Phase of Learning	Example Instructional Strategies
Surface level learning of the terms: natural resources, power, scarcity	• Vocabulary instruction of *natural resources* • Wide reading about natural resources • Summarizing understanding of natural resources • Repeating above strategies with the terms of *power* and *scarcity*
Surface level learning of primary and secondary source analysis	• Teacher modeling source analysis using IREAD strategy (Monte-Sano et al., 2014) • Teacher providing feedback on source analysis • Jigsaw strategy with sources on the Nile river
Deep level learning about power, resources, and scarcity on the Nile as well as source analysis	• Completing graphic organizers about power, resources, and scarcity on the Nile River • Close reading of differing opinion articles about the situation on the Nile River • Engaging in a class discussion to generalize about the relationships between and among these concepts • Thinking metacognitively about their understanding of the relationship
Transfer level of learning about power, resources, and scarcity as well as source analysis to new situations	• Students compare similarities and differences between the Nile river situations and another situation where resources, scarcity, and power play a role, such as the Tigris river that flows through Turkey and Iraq. • Students debate about the role of international groups where resources become scarce • Students compose an essay about an international conflict among scarce resources and make recommendations about solving the problem

Figure 1.1

The following year, Doug's world history class was very different. Like the year before, we read a textbook. We also read many primary source documents. The teacher scheduled frequent short lectures. We created concept maps. We had debates. We put world leaders, portrayed by the teacher, on trial. We wrote essays in which we had to make a claim and support it. One memorable unit required that we explain the phrase: The sun never sets on the British Empire. We had to discuss the literal and figurative meanings of the phrase, identify if this was ever true, and note whether it remained true today.

How much history do you think Doug remembers? From which experience? What type of learning experiences work best to help accelerate learning and deepen understanding that can be applied to new situations? This book strives to answer that question, drawing on a very large database about what works best to improve students' learning.

We have chosen the term social studies as we hope it serves as an umbrella term for the various aspects of the study of human society. This includes all of the content that students need to learn related to history, geography, economics, civics, anthropology, sociology, government systems, and political science—and we've included examples from kindergarten to grade 12. Yes, it's a lot and it's foundational to the ways in which people interact with each other, their communities, and the world at large. We would be remiss if we didn't include the words of George Santayana: "Those who cannot remember the past are condemned to repeat it." In other words, society's progress is dependent on members of the community to know their past and to recognize the social systems in place in a society.

The Evidence Base

The starting point for our exploration of social studies learning is John Hattie's books, *Visible Learning* (2009) and *Visible Learning for Teachers* (2012). At the time these books were published, his work was based on over 800 meta-analyses conducted by researchers all over the world, which included over 50,000 individual studies that included over 250 MILLION students. It has been claimed to be the most comprehensive review of literature ever conducted. And the thing is, it's still going on. At the time of this writing, the database includes 1,800 meta-analyses, with over 90,000 studies and 300 *million* students. A lot of data, right? But the story underlying the data is the critical matter.

Before we explore the findings and discuss what we don't cover in this book, we should discuss the idea of a meta-analysis because it is the basic building block for the recommendations in this book. At its root, a meta-analysis is a statistical tool for combining findings from different studies with the goal of identifying patterns that can inform practice. It's the old preponderance of evidence that we're looking for, because individual studies have a hard time making a compelling case for change. But a meta-analysis synthesizes what is currently known about a given topic and can result in strong recommendations about the impact or effect of a specific practice.

EFFECT SIZE
FOR CLASSROOM
DISCUSSION = 0.82

The statistical approach for conducting meta-analyses is beyond the scope of this book, but it is important to note that this tool allows researchers to identify trends across many different studies and their participants. For example, Murphy, Wilkinson, Soter, Hennessey, and Alexander (2009) conducted a meta-analysis on classroom discussion. They combined the findings from 39 studies that had over 84,000 participants. They note that there are some discussion approaches that are more effective than others, but that "talk appears to play a fundamental role in text-based comprehension" (p. 761). Given that, it seems reasonable to suggest that teachers integrate talk into their classrooms. Before you put down this book and run back to class to get students to talk about what they are reading, we caution that many of the instructional strategies found in the research work best *at a specific phase of learning*. As we will see, classroom discussion is particularly effective for deep learning but doesn't do much good for surface learning. More on these distinctions soon. For now, let's keep focused on the evidence.

Many of the instructional strategies found in the Visible Learning research work best *at a specific phase of learning*.

Effect Sizes

In addition to the meta-analyses, the largest summary of educational research ever conducted (*Visible Learning*) contains *effect sizes* for each practice. An effect size is the magnitude, or size, of a given effect. But defining a phrase by using the same terms isn't that helpful. So we'll try again. You might remember from your statistics class that studies report statistical significance. Researchers make the case that something *worked* when chance is reduced to 5 percent (as in p < .05) or 1 percent (as in

$p < .01$)—what they really mean is that the effect that was found in the study was unlikely to be zero: something happened (but no hint of the size of the effect, nor whether it was worthwhile!). One way to increase the likelihood that statistical significance is reached is to increase the number of people in the study, also known as sample size. We're not saying that researchers inflate the size of the research group to obtain significant findings. We are saying that simply because something is statistically significant doesn't mean that it's worth implementing. For example, say the sample size was 1,000, then a correlation only needs to exceed 0.044 to be *statistically significant*; if 10,000 then 0.014, and if 100,000 then 0.004—yes, you can be confident that these values are greater than zero, but are they of any practical value?

That's where effect size comes in.

Say, for example, that this amazing computer program was found to be statistically significant in changing student achievement. Sounds good, you say to yourself, and you consider purchasing or adopting it. But then you learn that it only increased students' performance by 3 points on a summative assessment (and the research team had data from 10,000 students). If it were free and easy to implement this change, it might be worth it to have students get a tiny bit better scores. But if it were time-consuming, difficult, or expensive, you should ask yourself if it's worth it to go to all of this trouble for such a small gain. That's effect size—it represents the magnitude of the impact that a given approach has. We think about it like the Richter scale, which is used to measure earthquakes. In California, we have about 10,000 earthquakes per year. But we don't feel all of them because their impact is small. They register very low on the Richter scale. In the language of learning, they have a very minimal effect.

Visible Learning provides readers with effect sizes for many influences under investigation. As an example, classroom discussion has a reasonably strong effect size at 0.82 (we'll talk more about what the effect size number tells us in the next section). The effect sizes can be ranked from those with the highest impact to those with the lowest. But that doesn't mean that teachers should just take the top 10 or 20 and try to implement them immediately. Rather, as we will discuss later in this book, some of the highly useful practices are more effective when focused on surface level learning while others work better for deep learning and still others work to encourage transfer. Purpose, context, and timing of practices all matter and must be considered. For more information on effect sizes, visit the companion website at http://resources.corwin.com/VL-socialstudies.

Noticing What Works

If you attend any conference or read just about any professional journal, not to mention subscribe to blogs or visit Pinterest, you'll get the sense that everything works.

Yet educators have a lot to learn from practices that do not work. In fact, we would argue that learning from what doesn't work, and not repeating those mistakes, is a valuable use of time. To determine what doesn't work, we turn our attention to effect sizes again.

Effect sizes can be negative or positive, and they scale from low to high. Intuitively, an effect size of 0.60 is better than an effect size of 0.20. Intuitively, we should welcome any effect that is greater than 0—as 0 means *no growth* and clearly any negative effect-size means a negative growth. If only it was this simple.

It turns out that about 95 percent plus of the influences that we use in schools have a positive effect; that is, the effect size of nearly everything we do is greater than zero. This helps explain why so many people can argue *with evidence* that their pet project works. If you set the bar at showing any growth above zero, it is indeed hard to find programs and practices that don't work. As described in *Visible Learning* (2009), we have to reject the starting point of zero. Students naturally mature and develop over the course of a year and thus actions, activities, and interventions that teachers use should *extend learning beyond what a student can achieve by simply attending school for a year.*

This is why John Hattie set the bar of acceptability higher—at the average of all the influences he compiled—from the home, parents, schools,

Actions, activities, and interventions that teachers use should *extend learning beyond what a student can achieve by simply attending school for a year.*

teachers, curricula, and teaching strategies. This average was 0.40 and Hattie called it the *hinge point*. He then undertook to study the underlying attributes that would explain why those influences higher than 0.40 had such a positive impact compared with those lower than 0.40. His findings were the impetus for the *Visible Learning* story.

Borrowing from *Visible Learning*, the barometer and hinge point are effective in explaining what we focus on in this book and why. Here's an example of how this might play out:

Let's focus on 1:1 technology initiatives, which are popular in some circles. In essence, students are taught using a laptop or tablet. This is an expensive intervention and yet one that parents feel is important, as computers are part of the world today. And there are sales people who claim that learning accelerates and there are testimonials about the students engaging in learning using devices. School systems have spent millions on technology. That's where the meta-analyses and effect size efforts can teach us. The barometer and hinge point for one-on-one laptops are presented in Figure 1.2. Note that at 0.16 this influence rests in the zone of *developmental effects*, which is below the average teacher effects and better than reverse effects. In other words, the evidence suggests that this has a limited influence on student learning. The technology might make it easier to store documents and provide access to materials, sure. But there isn't evidence that this is an accelerator of learning.

> EFFECT SIZE FOR 1:1 LAPTOPS = 0.16

Our focus in *Visible Learning for Social Studies* is on actions that fall inside the *zone of desired effects*, which is 0.40 and above. When actions are in the range of 0.40 and above, the data suggest that the effort extends beyond that which was expected from attending school for a year.

CAUTION. That does not mean that everything below 0.40 effect size is not worthy of attention. In fact, there are likely some useful approaches for teaching and learning that are not above this average. For example, collaborative learning has an effect size of 0.34, almost ensuring that students gain a year's worth of achievement for a year of education.

BAROMETER FOR THE INFLUENCE OF 1:1 LAPTOPS

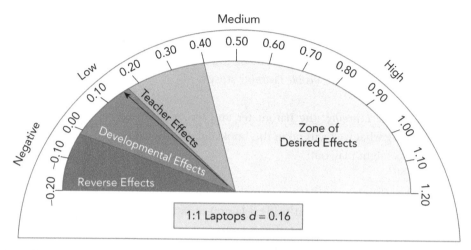

Source: Adapted from Hattie (2012).

Figure 1.2

We are not suggesting that collaborative learning be removed from the classroom. We are suggesting that it probably should not be the only thing that a teacher does to ensure deep learning. Another critical finding was the very low effect of teacher's subject matter knowledge. While we may accept the evidence that it is currently of little import, surely this means we should worry and investigate, first, why it is so low; and second, how we can change what we do in the classroom to ensure that the knowledge teachers bring to the classroom has a much higher effect.

It is important to note that some of the aggregate scores mask situations in which specific actions can be strategically used to improve students' understanding.

> EFFECT SIZE FOR SIMULATIONS = 0.34

Simulations are a good case. The effect size of simulations is 0.34, below the threshold that we established. But, what if simulations were really effective in deepening understanding but really, really bad when used with surface learning? In this case, the strategic deployment of simulations could be important. There are situations like this that we will review in this book as we focus on surface level learning versus deep learning and transfer learning. For now, let's turn our attention to actions that teachers can take to improve student learning.

Learning From What Works

The majority of this book will focus on learning social studies, specifically. In this next section, however, we focus our attention more broadly. The learning of social studies is situated in a larger classroom environment and is contextualized in the general learning situations that students encounter. We believe that the following influences deserve attention from teachers in all classes, including those devoted to social studies.

Teacher Credibility

A few things come to mind when we consider actions that teachers can take at the more generic level. On the top of the list with an effect size of 1.09 is teacher credibility. Students know which teachers can make a difference in their lives. Teacher credibility is a constellation of characteristics, including trust, competence, dynamism, and immediacy. Students evaluate each of these factors to determine if their teacher is credible, and if they are going to choose to learn from that teacher. Teachers can compromise their credibility when they violate trust, make a lot of errors, sit in the back of the room, or lack a sense of urgency. They compromise their credibility particularly if they are not seen to be fair.

EFFECT SIZE
FOR TEACHER
CREDIBILITY = 1.09

Of course, each of these needs to be held in balance. For example, too much pressure and students will think that a given teacher is a stress-case. Not enough and they think their teacher doesn't care. Similarly, students might think a teacher is weird when they fake excitement about a topic of study or realize that their teacher doesn't care about the unit at all. Although not specifically focused on social studies, the dynamic of teacher credibility is always at play.

Consider Angela Conner. She's always excited about everything. She knows her content well and works to establish trusting relationships with her students. But every time something happens, it's as if it's the most important and exciting thing ever. She is over the top with enthusiasm. This worked well for her with her kindergarten students, but her fifth graders think she's a fake. As one of the students said, "Yeah, Ms. Conner pretends to be excited, even when we get a test back. Really? It's important, but it's not like she should be jumping around like she does." This student and likely many more are questioning Ms. Conner's credibility and thus compromising their ability to learn from her.

On the other hand, Brandon Chu exudes excitement episodically and his students wait for it. Certain things seem very important to Mr. Chu. He tells his students why they are important and explains how the class builds on itself over the course of the year. In one lesson, Mr. Chu said, "We've got some pressure on us to get some major work done. It's crunch time, people, and we need to support each other in our learning. Please make sure that each of you has completed the concept map [effect size 0.64] and are ready to write. If you haven't had a peer review yet, let me know. We need to get these done so that they can be included in the upcoming e-zine. If we miss the deadline, we're out of the issue." Mr. Chu's students trust him and know when it's time to focus. They appreciate his dynamic, yet not overzealous style. And, importantly, they learn a lot.

Teacher–Student Relationships

EFFECT SIZE FOR TEACHER–STUDENT RELATIONSHIPS = 0.48

Closely related to teacher credibility are teacher–student relationships, which have an effect size of 0.48. When students believe that the teacher is credible, they are more likely to develop positive relationships with that teacher, and then learn more from him or her. But relationships go deeper than credibility. Of course, relationships are based on trust, which is part of the credibility construct. But relationships also require effective communication and addressing issues that strain the relationship. Positive relationships are fostered and maintained when teachers set fair expectations, involve students in determining aspects of the classroom organization and management, and hold students accountable for the expectations in an equitable way. Importantly, relationships are not destroyed when problematic behaviors occur, either on the part of the teacher or students. This is an important point for all educators. If we want to ensure students read, write, communicate, and think at high levels, we have to develop positive, trusting relationships with students, all students.

Optimal relationships develop when the teacher establishes high levels of trust with and among students. When a student asks a question indicating they are lost, do not know where they are going, or are just plain wrong, high levels of peer-to-peer trust means that this student is not ridiculed, does not feel that they should be silent and bear their not-knowing, and can depend on the teacher and often other students to help them out.

Video 1.1
Teacher–Student Relationships That Impact Learning

http://resources.corwin.com/ VL-socialstudies

Unfortunately, in some cases, specific students are targeted for behavioral correction while other students engaged in the same behavior are not noticed. This happens often across the K–12 grade span. We remember a primary grade classroom in which a student with a disability was repeatedly chastised for a problematic behavior, but then other children engaged in the same behavior were ignored and allowed to continue. Yes, the children noticed. As one of the students said, "Mr. Henderson doesn't want Michael in our class." It's hard to develop positive relationships, and then achieve, when you are not wanted. But, perhaps even more importantly, the poor relationship between Mr. Henderson and Michael spilled over to the rest of the students who didn't think their teacher was fair or that he was trustworthy.

We have also observed this phenomenon in secondary classrooms. There always seem to be some students who can get away with problematic behavior. Sometimes, these students are athletes, other times cheerleaders or drama students or musicians or students whose parents work in the district. It doesn't really matter which group they belong to, their status allows them to get away with things that other students don't. And it always compromises the trust students have with their teacher and the relationships that develop.

But we're not saying that educators should be strict disciplinarians who mete out punishments and consequences for every infraction. We are saying that it's important to be consistent, fair, and to repair relationships that are damaged when problematic behavior occurs. To develop positive relationships, it's important that teachers do the following:

- Display student work

- Share class achievements

- Speak to the accomplishments of all students

- Be sincere in your pride in your students and make sure that pride is based on evidence of student work, not generalized comments

- Look for opportunities for students to be proud of themselves and of other students or groups of students

- Develop parental pride in student accomplishments

- Develop pride in improvement in addition to pride in excellence

We've spent time on this because relationships matter and students achieve more and better when they develop strong interpersonal relationships with their teachers. It's these humane and growth-producing conversations that help students grow in their prosocial behaviors. (Note, that the greatest effect on achievement when a student joins a new class or school is related to whether they make a friend in the first month—it is your job to worry about friendship, counter loneliness, and help students gain a reputation as a great learner not only in your eyes but also in the eyes of their peers.) And by the way, effectively managed classrooms, ones in which students understand the expectations and are held to those expectations in ways that are consistent with relationship development and maintenance, has an effect size of 0.35. A poorly run classroom will interfere with high quality learning.

Teacher Expectations

EFFECT SIZE FOR TEACHER EXPECTATIONS = 0.43

Another influence on student achievement that is important for educators is teacher expectations, with an effect size of 0.43. In large part, teachers get what they expect; yes teachers with low expectations are particularly successful at getting what they expect. The more recent research has shown that teachers who have high (or low) expectations tend to have them for all their students (Rubie-Davies, 2015). Teachers' expectations become the reality for students. A kindergarten teacher who expects students to understand temporal order and be able to place days, weeks, and months in the proper order will likely have students accomplish that goal. A high school history teacher who expects students to develop habits of debate and to argue with evidence will likely produce students who can do so. Hattie (2012) called this the *minimax* principle, "maximum grade return for minimal extra effort" (p. 93). And it gets in the way of better and deeper learning. When expectations are high, the minimax principle can work to facilitate students' learning.

This does not mean that teachers should set unrealistic expectations. Telling first graders that they are required to memorize the names of all of the state capitals is a bit too far. Teachers should have expectations that appropriately stretch students, and yet those expectations should be within reach. Sixth graders who are held to fourth grade expectations will be great fifth graders when they are in seventh grade; the gap never closes. And students deserve more. When high yield instructional routines are utilized, students can achieve more than a year's growth during a year of instruction. And that's what this book focuses on—maximizing the impact teachers have on students' learning.

Establishing and communicating a learning intention is an important way that teachers share their expectations with students. When these learning intentions are compared with grade-level expectations, or expectations in other schools and districts, educators can get a sense of their appropriateness. We will spend a lot more time later in this book focused on learning intentions and success criteria. Another way to assess the level of expectation is to invite students to share their goals for learning with their teachers—especially early in the instructional sequence. If students have low expectations for themselves, they're likely hearing that from the adults around them, and often this is what they achieve. And finally, analyzing the success criteria is an important way of determining the expectations a teacher has for students. A given

> Teachers' expectations become the reality for students.

learning intention could have multiple success criteria, some of which may be fairly low and others of which may be high. The success criteria communicates the level of performance that students are expected to meet, yet is often overlooked in explorations about teacher expectations. We'll return to success criteria in the next section of this chapter, but before we do so, it's important to note that teachers establish expectations in other ways beyond the learning intention.

The ways in which teachers consciously and subconsciously communicate their expectations to students are too numerous to list. Expectations are everywhere, in every exchange teachers and students have. When teachers use academic language in their interactions with others, they communicate their expectations. When teachers maintain a clean and inviting classroom, they communicate their expectations. When teachers assign mindless shut-up sheets, they communicate their expectations. When teachers provide honest feedback about students' work, they communicate their expectations.

When teachers give one class two days to complete work and another class one day, they communicate their expectations. We could go on. Students watch their teachers all the time, trying to figure out what is expected of them and if they are trustworthy. Learning can be enhanced when teachers communicate specific, relevant, and appropriate expectations for students. From there, teachers can design amazing learning environments. But it's more than instruction. Teachers should focus on *learning*. It's a mind-set that we all need, if we are going to ensure that students develop their literate selves. A major theme throughout this book is about how teachers think (and also how we want students to think). Hattie (2012) suggests ten mindframes that can be used to guide decisions, from curriculum adoptions to lesson planning (Figure 1.3).

Video 1.2
Mindframes of
Assessment-Capable
Teachers

*http://resources.corwin.com/
VL-socialstudies*

Taken together, these mindframes summarize a great deal of the *what works* literature. In the remainder of this book, we focus on putting these into practice specifically as they relate to social studies learning, and address the better question: *what works best?* (Hattie, 2009) To do so, we need to consider the levels of learning we can expect from students.

MINDFRAMES FOR TEACHERS

1. I cooperate with other teachers.

2. I use dialogue not monologue.

3. I set the challenge.

4. I talk about learning not teaching.

5. I inform all about the language of learning.

6. I see learning as hard work.

7. Assessment is feedback to me about me.

8. I am a change agent.

9. I am an evaluator.

10. I develop positive relationships.

Figure 1.3

How then should we define learning, since that is our goal? As John himself suggested, learning can be defined as

> [t]he process of developing sufficient surface knowledge to then move to deeper understanding such that one can appropriately transfer this learning to new tasks and situations.

Learning is a process, not an event. And there is a scale for learning. Some things, students only understand at the surface level. As we note in the next chapter, surface learning is not valued, but it should be. You have to know something to be able to do something with it. We've never met a student who could synthesize information from multiple primary and secondary sources who didn't have an understanding of each of the texts. With appropriate instruction about how to relate and extend ideas, surface learning becomes deep understanding. Deep understanding is important if students are going to set their own expectations and monitor their own achievement (effect size 1.33). But schooling should not stop there. Learning demands that students be able to apply—transfer—their knowledge, skills, and strategies to new tasks and new situations. That transfer is so difficult to attain is one of our closely kept secrets—so often we pronounce students can transfer but the processes of teaching them this skill is too often not discussed. We will discuss it in Chapter 4.

Unfortunately, up to 90 percent of the instruction we conduct can be completed by students using *only* the surface level skills (Hattie, 2012). Read that sentence carefully—it did not say that teachers do not ask students to complete deeper analyses and it did not say that teachers do not ask students to complete tests and assignments that focus on deeper learning. It said that students only need a high level of surface level knowledge to do well on this work. Why? Because despite teachers preaching deeper learning, the instruction we conduct does not match this value. We need to balance our expectations with our reality. This means more constructive alignment between what teachers claim success looks like, how the tasks students are assigned align with these claims about success, and how success is measured by end of course assessments or assignments. It is not a matter of all surface or deep, it is a matter of being clear when surface and when deep is truly required.

The ultimate goal, and one that is hard to realize, is transfer (see Figure 1.4).

When students reach this level, learning has been accomplished. One challenge to this model is that most assessments focus on surface level learning because that level is easier to evaluate. But, as David Coleman, president of the College Board, said, test makers have to assume responsibility for the practice their assessment inspires. That applies to all of us. If the assessment focuses on recall, then a great number of instructional minutes will be devoted to developing students' ability to demonstrate *learning* that way.

What and *when* are equally important when it comes to instruction that has an impact on learning.

As teachers, we are faced with a wide range of assessments that are used to evaluate student achievement and teacher performance. But these come and go. Teachers also make tests and should assume responsibility for the practices that result from their own creations.

In this book, we devote time to each level or phase of learning. Importantly, there are teacher and student actions that work best at

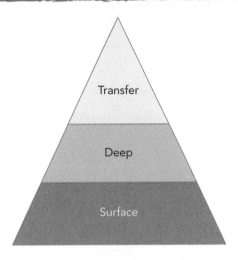

Figure 1.4

each of these phases. For example, note-taking works well for surface level learning whereas class discussions and close reading probably work better for deep learning. A key point that we will make repeatedly is that teachers have to understand the impact that they have on students, and choose approaches that will maximize that impact. Mismatching an approach with the level of learning expected will not create the desired impact. *What* and *when* are equally important when it comes to instruction that has an impact on learning.

Video 1.3
The Right Strategy at the Right Time: Surface, Deep, and Transfer Learning

http://resources.corwin.com/ VL-socialstudies

General Learning Practices

Before we dive into the levels of learning as they relate to social studies, there are three aspects of learning that transcend the three-phase model:

1. Challenge

2. Self-efficacy

3. Learning intentions with success criteria

These should be considered in each and every learning situation, as they are global factors that impact understanding. We will explain each of these in more detail below.

1. Challenge

The first of these global aspects is challenge. Students appreciate challenge.

They expect to work hard to achieve success in school and life. When tasks become too easy, students get bored. Similarly, when tasks become too difficult, students get frustrated. There is a sweet spot for learning, but the problem is that it differs for different students. There is a Goldilocks notion of not making a task too easy (or too boring), or too hard. It needs to be just right. As Tomlinson (2005) noted,

> Ensuring challenge is calibrated to the particular needs of a learner at a particular time is one of the most essential roles of the teacher and appears non-negotiable for student growth. Our best understanding suggests that a student only learns when work is moderately challenging that student, and where there is assistance to help the student master what initially seems out of reach. (pp. 163–164)

How then can educators keep students challenged but not frustrated? There are several responses to this question, and our answer is embedded in every chapter of this book. In part, we would respond that the type of learning intention is important to maintain challenge.

Surface, Deep, or Transfer

The teacher should know if students need surface, deep, or transfer type work—or what combination—while ensuring the parts are explicit for the student. In this way, the teacher can maintain the challenge while providing appropriate instructional supports.

Showing students near the beginning of a series of lessons what success at the end should look like is among the more powerful things we can do to enhance learning. There are many ways to do this, including

- showing them worked examples of an A, B, and C piece of work, and discussing how they differ;

- giving them the scoring rubrics at the outset and teaching them what they mean;

- sharing last year's students' work in the same series of lessons; and

- building a concept map with them up front to show the interrelationships between the various parts they will learn about.

These tools help provide a coat hanger for students to know what good enough is, what success looks like, and how they will know when they get there. Not showing this is like asking a high jumper to jump the bar but not telling or showing them how high the bar is!

Student-to-Student Interaction

In addition, we would add that schools should be filled with student-to-student interaction. As one of the mind frames (Figure 1.2) suggests, classrooms should be filled with dialogue rather than monologues. We say this for several reasons, including the fact that no one gets good at something they don't do. If students aren't using language—speaking, listening, reading, and writing—they're not likely to excel in those areas.

Further, as students work collaboratively and cooperatively (which has an effect size of 0.55) rather than individualistically, the assigned tasks can be more complex because there are many minds at work on solving the tasks. Of course, this requires clear expectations for group work and instruction about how to work with others. But the outcomes are worth it—students learn more deeply when they are engaged in complex tasks that involve collaboration (they don't necessarily learn more from collaborating with others when the learning focuses on surface level content). Further, when students work together in groups, they have an opportunity to engage in peer tutoring, which has an effect size of 0.51.

2. Self-Efficacy

A second global consideration for educators is students' self-efficacy. Hattie (2012) defines self-efficacy as "the confidence or strength of

EFFECT SIZE FOR STUDENT SELF-EFFICACY = 0.71

belief that we have in ourselves that we can make our learning happen" (p. 45). He continues, with descriptions of students with high self-efficacy, noting that they

- understand complex tasks as challenges rather than trying to avoid them;
- experience failure as opportunities to learn, which may require additional effort, information, support, time, and so on; and
- quickly recover a sense of confidence after setbacks.

By contrast, students with low self-efficacy

- avoid complex and difficult tasks (as these are seen as personal threats),
- maintain weak commitment to goals,
- experience failure as a personal deficiency, and
- slowly recover a sense of confidence after setbacks.

It almost goes without saying that the impact of self-efficacy on learning is significant. Our emotions, the sense of failure, and our anxieties are often invoked in our learning—or more often in our resistance to engage in learning. Building a sense of confidence that you can indeed attain the criteria of success for the lessons may be a first critical step—without a sense of confidence, we often do not open our ears to what we are being taught. Most of us are more likely to engage in difficult, complex, or risky learning if we know there is help nearby, that there are safety nets, that we will not be ridiculed if we do not succeed—this is where the power of the teacher lies.

Students with high self-efficacy perform better and understand that their efforts can result in better learning. This becomes a self-fulfilling prophecy: the rich get richer and the poor get poorer. Students with poor self-efficacy see each challenge and setback as evidence that they aren't learning, and in fact can't learn, which reduces the likelihood that they will rally the forces for the next task the teacher assigns.

In their study about ways to increase students' self-efficacy, Mathisen and Bronnick (2009) suggested a combination of the following (each of which is addressed later in this book in more detail):

- Direct instruction with modeled examples

- Verbal persuasion through introductory information

- Feedback on attempts made by learners

- Guided use of techniques on well-defined problems

- Supervised use of techniques on self-generated problems

To which we add the following:

- Demonstrating your credibility by being fair to all

- Being there to help students reach targets

- Creating high levels of trust between you and the students and between student and student

- Showing that you welcome errors as opportunities for learning

- Others have made different recommendations (e.g., Linnenbrink & Pintrich, 2003) and our point here is not to endorse one approach over another but rather to confirm that teachers can change students' agency and identity such that self-efficacy, the "belief that we have in ourselves that we can make our learning happen" (Hattie, 2012, p. 46), is fostered.

3. Learning Intentions With Success Criteria

The third and final global aspect that should permeate social studies learning relates to being explicit about the nature of learning that students are expected to do and the level of success expected from the lesson. Teacher clarity about learning expectations, including the ways in which students can demonstrate their understanding, is powerful.

The effect size is 0.75. Every lesson, irrespective of whether it focuses on surface, deep, or transfer, needs to have clearly articulated learning intentions and success criteria. We believe that students should be able to answer, and ask, these questions of each lesson:

1. What am I learning today?

2. Why am I learning this?

3. How will I know that I learned it?

The first question requires deep understanding of the learning intention. The second question begs for relevance, and the third question focuses on the success criteria. Neglecting any of these questions compromises students' learning. In fact, we argue that these questions compose part of the Learner's Bill of Rights. Given that teachers (and the public at large) judge students based on their performance, it seems only fair that students should know what they are expected to learn, why they are learning that, and how success will be determined. The marks teachers make on report cards and transcripts become part of the permanent record that follows students around. Those documents have the power to change parents' perceptions of their child, determine future placements in school, and open college doors.

We're not saying that it's easy to identify learning intentions and success criteria. Smith (2007) notes, "Writing learning intentions and success criteria is not easy . . . because it forces us to 'really, really think' about what we want the pupils to learn rather than simply accepting statements handed on by others" (p. 14). We are saying that it's worth the effort. Clearly articulating the goals for learning has an effect size of 0.50. It's the right thing to do, and it's effective.

Learning intentions are more than a standard. There have been far too many misguided efforts that mandated teachers to post the standard on the wall. Learning intentions are based on the standard, but are chunked into learning bites. In too many cases, the standards are not understandable to students. Learning intentions, if they are to be effective, have to be understood and accepted by students. Simply writing a target on the dry erase board and then reading it aloud waters down the power of a learning intention, which

SAMPLE LEARNING INTENTIONS

Grade	Improved Version
K	Today, we are going to think about our classroom community. We are going to learn about the roles and responsibilities we each have in this classroom community. We are also going to learn about the different roles and responsibilities we have based on our classroom jobs.
5	We are learning about profits and how the need to profit influences sellers. We will learn about the relationship between prices of goods or services and the profit sellers gain.
7	We are continuing our learning about trade routes. Today, we are learning about spice trading and some of the Asian routes.
11	Today we are learning about religious intolerance. We will explore the impact of this type of intolerance on people in several different societies and will identify common themes about religious intolerance.

Figure 1.5

should focus the entire lesson and serve as an organizing feature of the learning students do. At minimum, learning intentions should bookend lessons with clear communication about the learning target early in the lesson and later reference to it as the lesson closes. In addition, teachers can remind students of the learning intention at each transition point throughout the lesson. In this way, the learning intention drives the lesson and students will develop a better understanding of how close they are to mastering the expectations. Most critical, the learning intention should demonstrably lead to the criteria of success—and if you had to use only one of these, we would recommend focusing on being more explicit about the success criteria. Both help, but it is the judgment about the standard of work desired that is more important than explication about the particular tasks we ask students to do. It is the height of the bar, not the bar itself that matters.

Figure 1.5 contains some learning intentions that teachers created collaboratively as they explored the value of this approach. Note that they became longer, more specific, and more interesting. The improved versions invite students into learning. Of course, learning intentions can be grouped. Sometimes an activity can contribute to several learning intentions and other times a learning intention requires several activities.

However, when learning intentions are spread over many days, student interest will wane and motivation will decrease. When teachers plan a unit of instruction and clearly identify the learning intentions required for mastery of the content, most times they can identify daily targets. In doing so, they can also identify the success criteria, which will allow for checking for understanding and targeted feedback.

The success criteria must be directly linked with learning intentions to have any impact. The success criteria describe how students will be expected to demonstrate their learning, based on the learning intention. That's not to say that success criteria are just a culminating activity, but they can be. Consider the following ways that students might demonstrate success based on a learning intention that reads,

> *We are learning to analyze visual images presented in the text and determine how this information contributes to and clarifies information.*

- I can discuss with a partner the way the author used visuals and how the author helped me understand the text.

- I can identify one place in the text that was confusing and how one of the visuals helped me understand that information.

- I can include annotations that show where visual information helped me understand the text itself.

- I can create a visual that will help another person understand the words in the text.

All of these work, in different situations. Clarity is important here. What is it that students should be learning, and how will they know (not to mention how will the teacher know) if they learned it? That's the power of learning intentions and success criteria.

SAMPLE SELF-ASSESSMENT OF LEARNING

I do not yet understand. I need coaching.	I am starting to understand.
	I need coaching but want to try some on my own.
I understand!	I understand very well.
I make a few mistakes so I'm working through those.	I can explain this to others without telling them the answers.

Figure 1.6

Importantly, students can be involved in establishing the success criteria, and in many cases the learning intentions. Teachers can ask their students *"How will you know you have learned this? What evidence could we accept that learning has occurred?"* In these situations, students can share their thinking about the success criteria, and often they are more demanding of themselves than their teachers are. In a sixth-grade class focused on learning to come to group discussions prepared, the students identified several ways that they would know if they met this expectation. Several suggested that they should have their learning materials with them when they move into collaborative learning. Others added that they should have their notes and annotations updated and be ready to talk about their reading, rather than read while they are in the group. One student suggested that they should practice vocabulary before the group so that they would be ready. Another added that they should each know their role in the group so that they can get started right away. None of these answers are wrong; they're all useful in improving the collaborative learning time. In this case, the students established the success criteria and opened the door to feedback from the peers and the teacher in their successive approximations in demonstrating mastery of their learning.

Further, when students understand the success criteria, they can be more involved in assessing their own success, and their progression toward this success. A simple tool allows students to put sticky notes in one of four quadrants to communicate their status (see Figure 1.6). This alerts the teacher, and other students, about help that is needed. It mobilizes peer tutoring (with an effect size of 0.51), cooperative versus competitive

SAMPLE PROJECT CHECKLIST

Pamphlet portion		
Item	Date projected	Completed ✓
Cover has the title, image, and your name		
Description of your cause (minimum 10 sentences)		
List 3–5 important facts		
Map of where this is occurring		
Demographics of who/what is impacted		
Minimum of 3 images in your brochure		
Contact information (websites, telephone numbers)		
Upcoming events (celebrations, day, movie, anniversary date, races, etc.)		
Pamphlet is attractive and well organized		
Correct spelling and grammar		

Figure 1.7

learning (with an effect size of 0.53) as well as building student-centered teaching (with an effect size of 0.36).

Other times, the tools used to create the success criteria involve rubrics and checklists. For example, students in a high school civics class were tasked with selecting a worthy cause, something that they cared passionately about and could explain the value to others. Students were encouraged to select topics that were personally relevant and to learn more about that topic. As part of the assignment, students wrote an analytic essay about their chosen topic. Another part of the project required that they develop a webpage, Facebook page, or other electronic way of communicating with a wider world about their cause. And still another part of their assignment required the development of an informational pamphlet that they could use to educate adults about the issue. Students selected a range of worthy causes, from Islamaphobia to endangered animals to mental health. Figure 1.7 contains the checklist that the teachers used to communicate their expectations to students. Note that many of these are compliance-related items that will subsequently allow teachers, and students, to determine if the experience left a lasting impact. The teachers were aiming to tap into creativity efforts (with an effect size of 0.64) and integrated curricular approaches (with an effect size of 0.47). They were also looking for evidence of learning transfer, asking students to mobilize their skills for a task they had not completed before.

Clearly articulating the success criteria allows errors to become more obvious. Errors should be expected and celebrated because they are opportunities for learning. If students are not making errors, they have likely previously mastered the learning intention. Also note that feedback thrives on the presence of errors. Errors should be the hallmark of learning—if we are not making enough errors, we are not stretching ourselves; if we make too many, we need more help to start in a different place.

Unfortunately, in too many classrooms, students who already know the content are privileged and students who make errors feel shame. In those situations, learning isn't occurring for students who already know the content; they've already learned it. But learning isn't occurring for the students who make errors because they hide their errors and avoid feedback. Classrooms have to be safe places for errors to be recognized.

Video 1.4
Viewing Errors
as Opportunities

*http://resources.corwin.com/
VL-socialstudies*

For example, a secondary world history class was focused on creating posters to review the Colombian exchange—there were images and glue sticks everywhere, with students printing and cutting out pictures of crops, animals, and cultural artifacts along with images of slavery and disease, some of which were historically accurate to the period of Columbus and some of which were not. But when they were asked how long had they being doing this task, they said two weeks (and that they enjoyed the project). What a waste of a week or more. Perfection is not necessarily the aim of lessons; the presence of errors is a better indicator of a successful lesson, and surely hints to the teacher and student where is the most likely place to go next.

FEEDBACK STRATEGIES

Feedback Strategies Can Vary In . . .	In These Ways . . .	Recommendations for Good Feedback
Timing	• When given • How often	• Provide immediate feedback for knowledge of facts (right/wrong). • Delay feedback slightly for more comprehensive reviews of student thinking and processing. • Never delay feedback beyond when it would make a difference to students. • Provide feedback as often as is practical, for all major assignments.
Amount	• How many points made • How much about each point	• Prioritize—pick the most important points. • Choose points that relate to major learning goals. • Consider the student's developmental level.
Mode	• Oral • Written • Visual/ demonstration	• Select the best mode for the message. Would a comment in passing the student's desk suffice? Is a conference needed? • Interactive feedback (talking with the student) is best when possible. • Give written feedback on written work or on assignment cover sheets. • Use demonstration if *how to do something* is an issue or if the student needs an example.
Audience	• Individual • Group/class	• Individual feedback says, "The teacher values my learning." • Group/class feedback works if most of the class missed the same concept on an assignment, which presents an opportunity for reteaching.

online resources Available for download at **http://resources.corwin.com/VL-socialstudies**

Figure 1.8

When errors are celebrated and expected, feedback takes hold. Feedback has a powerful impact on student learning, with an effect size of 0.66. But it's only when the feedback is received that it works. Giving feedback is different from receiving feedback. Feedback is designed to close the gap between students' current level of understanding or performance and the expected level of performance, which we call the success criteria.

EFFECT SIZE FOR
FEEDBACK = 0.66

For feedback to work, teachers have to understand

- students' current level of performance;

- students' expected level of performance; and

- actions they can take to close the gap.

Feedback, as Brookhart (2008) describes it, needs to be "just-in-time, just-for-me information delivered when and where it can do the most good" (p. 1). Figure 1.8 includes information about the ways in which feedback can vary in terms of timing, amount, mode, and audience. We'll focus on feedback in greater depth in the chapter on deep learning. For now, we hope you appreciate the value of feedback in impacting student learning.

Conclusion

Teachers, we have choices. We can elect to use instructional routines and procedures that don't work, or don't work for the intended purpose. Or we can embrace the evidence, update our classrooms, and impact student learning in wildly positive ways. We can choose to move beyond surface level learning, while still honoring the importance of teaching students surface level concepts, skills, and strategies. We can extend students' learning in deep ways and facilitate the transfer of their learning to new tasks, texts, and projects, if we want. We can design amazing lessons that mobilize the evidence and provide opportunities for students to learn. And we can decide to evaluate our impact, if we are brave enough.

We know a student named Monica who struggled with social studies at a school where teachers did not consider the appropriate strategy to match the specific phase of the learning journey. Nor did they teach Monica how to monitor her own learning or to think like a disciplinarian in social studies. Monica was lucky enough to transfer to a school that embraced *Visible Learning*. Her teachers tried out the instructional ideas, monitored progress, and provided feedback to her and to each other. Monica went from a failing student, tracked in a class with low expectations, to a lead learner providing support for her peers. Impact has a face. It's not an abstract idea or ideal. Together, we can impact the learning of every student. Let's make it so.

SURFACE LEARNING IN SOCIAL STUDIES

2

The phrase *surface learning* holds a negative connotation for many people. Teachers are hesitant to acknowledge that anything they do is at the surface level. But this is wrongheaded and dismisses the essential practice of a strong start. Consider the deep wells of knowledge and skills you possess about your professional practice. Now recall how it began. In all likelihood, it began formally in your teacher preparation program, but it certainly didn't stop there. Over time, you have been able to craft that initial knowledge into a broader and deeper set of practices that allow you to respond effectively to new and novel situations. It is about getting the balance between surface, deep, and transfer right. It's not about privileging one over the others.

Learning has to begin somewhere. Like a swimmer entering the water, the initial steps require breaking the surface. Nothing else can occur if the entry never happens. As well, a strong beginning sets the stage for later success. And because social studies learning involves complex, disciplinary literacy skills such as analyzing primary and secondary sources and composing arguments, the swimming analogy is a particularly strong one for us to use.

Consider Mr. Jackson, a Grade 1 teacher who is beginning a unit on roles and responsibilities. He combines this learning outcome with a

> It is about getting the balance between surface, deep, and transfer right. It's not about privileging one over the others.

33

disciplinary literacy standard of determining reliable sources, a learning outcome found in many state and provincial standards or outcomes documents as well as in the C3 Framework (National Council for the Social Studies, 2013, p. 25). By the end of the unit, he wants students to understand the responsibility of citizens and to distinguish between reliable and unreliable information—lofty goals for Grade 1, but achievable when the learning environment is structured well. Notice how he sets the stage for this from the start, gradually but efficiently and effectively helping students acquire and consolidate their understanding of these ideas.

Mr. Jackson begins with a series of pictures from the school's own community and asks students to identify the different types of people, as well as describe the part they play in helping us to learn—such as students, teachers, principals, librarians, bus drivers, custodians, counselors, coaches, parents, etc. He explains that there is a word for the *part they play* in the school community, and writes it up on the board: *role*. After the students have practiced using the word *role* to describe one of the pictures, he conducts a similar activity with class responsibilities that are familiar to students—such as treating our classroom materials with care, washing paintbrushes, and wiping tables after art projects, etc.—to introduce the concept of *responsibility*.

Next, he reads a picture book aloud about different roles in the community, *What Do People Do All Day?* (Scarry, 2015). During his read aloud, he pauses to model for students how he connects what the story is saying to the word *role*. After modeling a couple of examples, he asks if any student would like to give this a try. He provides the sentence frames he used, "I'm noticing that . . ." and "I think this relates to the word 'role' because . . ." After a few students try it out for the class, he asks all students to try it out with their partners.

He has consulted with the school librarian to gather several picture books about roles and responsibilities. In small groups, he asks students to select a book and try to find a picture that shows an example of someone who is playing a particular *role* and an example of a picture that shows *responsibility* with their partner. He also reviews a previous unit's learning on identifying the text features such as headings and illustrations with these same books.

Now that students have acquired surface level learning of roles and responsibilities, it is time for them to consolidate their learning. A few days later, he gives students images of people such as a fire fighter, police officer, etc., and asks them to name and describe the role they see and the responsibility each person has for the community. Finally, he asks students to name some different roles they have such as student, sibling, child, pet owner, friend, cousin, etc. He divides them into groups and assigns them one of these roles. In this expert group, they come up with an explanation of the role and an example of a corresponding responsibility they have in the assigned role. Then they move to new groups where each child takes turns to explain the role and responsibility they had from their original groups.

Mr. Jackson invested in several teaching strategies to ensure students acquired and consolidated their understanding of the concepts of role and responsibility. Now, they are ready to go deeper by becoming more conscious of their understanding of roles and responsibilities; and they will do this through exploring more complex areas where roles and responsibilities interplay. We need surface learning to be able to relate, extend, and think deeply. It is a matter of proportion—when we first are exposed to something, we need more surface learning; as we get more surface knowledge, we move to deep learning. See Figure 2.1 for a chart outlining the strategies presented in this example.

In this chapter, we will examine the importance of surface learning in social studies and consider the use of high-impact approaches that foster initial acquisition and consolidation. As we noted in the first chapter, almost everything in published research works at least some of the time with some students. Our challenge as a profession is to become more precise in what we do and when we do it. Timing is everything, and the wrong practice at the wrong time undermines efforts. Knowing when to help a student move from surface to deep is one of the marks of expert teachers. Teaching practices that foster deep learning, as discussed in the following chapter, are not the most effective ones to employ when students are still at the surface level of learning.

Knowing when to help a student move from surface to deep is one of the marks of expert teachers.

EXAMPLE INSTRUCTIONAL STRATEGIES OF SURFACE LEARNING

Example Instructional Strategies	What it Looks Like in the Classroom
Leveraging prior knowledge	• Students examining images of different roles and responsibilities in school to determine the critical attributes of each word
Teacher modeling	• Teacher demonstrating how he recognizes roles and responsibilities in texts
Wide reading	• Students reading and recognizing roles and responsibilities in a wide variety of texts
Spaced practice	• Students practicing identifying text features learned in a previous lesson • Students sorting and elaborating on examples of roles and responsibilities
Jigsaw	• Students form expert groups of various roles and responsibilities, then move to new groups to explain to their peers

Figure 2.1

Why Surface Learning Is Essential

EFFECT SIZE FOR PROBLEM-BASED LEARNING = 0.35

In retrospect, this was obvious, yet we didn't understand it at the time. Nancy recalls working with seasoned teachers to develop new knowledge and skills about problem-based learning (PBL). She held workshops, engaged in professional reading and discussions, and hosted a professional learning community focused on the practice. Yet time and again, the effort fizzled as teachers said it didn't work. They blamed their students' existing knowledge, lack of motivation, and inability to engage in self-directed learning. PBL, they said, didn't work, full stop. Yet problem-based learning can work, under the right conditions. However—and this is critical—it isn't particularly effective when students don't yet possess the knowledge, skills, and dispositions needed to engage in a more independent investigation into a topic. In other words, the timing is off. PBL is better for encouraging transfer, but not for the initial surface learning needed in advance of such inquiry.

Hattie (2009) refers to the phases of the learning journey as the worlds of "ideas, thinking, and constructing" (p. 26). He further reinterprets these three worlds as surface, deep, and transfer learning. There has been much deserved criticism of remaining at surface (some would say superficial) learning at the expense of learning that deepens over time and leads to transfer to new and novel situations. But how do we move efficiently through each phase of learning? We need to maximize precious instructional time with students—and this book helps us to know when to use which tools to do just that.

It's not that teachers jump too quickly to deeper learning. In fact, many of us need to change our understanding of surface level learning. Surface learning is not synonymous with recall; it's more complex than that. We often think we are starting at an introductory level, but we can focus attention on ways to start our units of instruction with more effective teaching strategies.

There are two common pitfalls that we need to consciously avoid during the surface or initial learning phase. The first is confusing surface level learning—an essential step—with rote learning, which is more or less starting with *memorization* of facts and details without any metacognitive or conscious awareness of what or why we are studying. An example of rote learning would be asking students to memorize capitals without beginning with at least initial discussion of the significance of capitals and a geographic awareness of where they are located. We are likely in the rote-learning zone when we ask students why they are learning what they are learning and the only answer they can give is "Because the teacher said so." The same idea here can be applied to starting with memorization of the name of leaders, geographic features of a place, or dates without first discussing why these are significant.

Memorization has its place in learning but it is usually not the opening activity of a new topic. It is useful for social studies teachers to think about the organizing idea, or concept, that frames a set of facts or details. For example, *leadership* or *authority* to frame the important people students should be able to readily identify. Or *geographic features* or *natural resources* to frame the important rivers, lakes, mountain ranges, etc., that we want students to recall from memory. Mr. Jackson, our Grade 1 example, focused on helping students understand the organizing idea of *role* and *responsibility* rather than starting with rote memorization of names of people and their roles in the community.

The second common pitfall relates to teaching for disciplinary literacy such as primary and secondary source analysis, interpretation, and contextualization. We often confuse lower-level questioning of students' disciplinary literacy skills with high-quality instruction of teaching them the steps involved in a complex skill. Let's return to Mr. Jackson's classroom to consider this point. When he introduces the disciplinary literacy practice of determining the reliability of sources, he begins by modeling how he can tell the difference between a book that tells a story and a book that gives information. He then asks students if they can explain the difference in their own words. A couple students relate the difference as books that are *pretend* and books that are *real*. He asks students why it might be important to distinguish between books that tell information and books that tell a story. One student exclaims, "So that we won't be scared of stories with ghosts or wolves that eat people, if we know they are just pretend stories." Another student says, "Some books are funny and make us to think silly things so we can laugh. Other books tell us information about real things so we can learn more, like about animals or the solar system." Another student explains, "Books that give information are books that have the truth." Several students then reference books they've previously read about the importance of telling the truth. Mr. Jackson uses these ideas to make a chart to compare the critical attributes of storybooks and informational books.

This teacher invests in activities that explore key attributes of the organizing disciplinary literacy concepts—in this case *storybooks* and *informational books*, before asking students to try to identify these on their own. Now they are ready to sort books into *story* and *information* and will likely notice there are some books that fit somewhere in between. But first, Mr. Jackson modeled his thinking, conducted intentional vocabulary instruction on these two concepts, and connected concepts with students' prior knowledge. These were necessary first steps before asking students to try out their understanding on their own. Social studies teachers must carefully plan our disciplinary literacy instruction as well as our content instruction. This book will continue to demonstrate ways to do both through the surface, deep, and transfer phases of learning.

In discussing common classroom efforts to teach students disciplinary literacy, Wineburg laments, "We throw young writers to the wolves, expecting them to absorb complex skills by osmosis" (cited in Monte-Sano et al., 2014, p. x). This applies to primary and secondary source analysis. A student isn't going to be able to evaluate two pieces of contradictory texts if she doesn't have a solid grounding in what each of the texts means at the literal, structural, and inferential levels. In other words, a student's ability to engage in analytical thinking can be inhibited if she hasn't had the opportunity to acquire and consolidate the surface knowledge and skills she will need.

Placing the right amount of emphasis at the right time in the instructional sequence is essential. Balance is warranted. Above all, social studies teachers need to be clear about their goals across learning units, recognize how these goals transform across time, and clearly communicate these goals to students. That means that within and across units, learning moves from surface level to deeper understanding, leading students to develop the ability to transfer knowledge and skills into new situations. As such, instruction needs to be attuned to where students are, and where they are headed, across these three major phases. Teachers pay a huge disservice to students when they stop the learning once the surface level is mastered.

In turn, we are equally at fault when we skim over this first phase and prematurely ask students to construct without the tools they need to do so. It also does not mean we have to bore students, make them rote learn, and just focus on facts or definitions. Note, for example, the meta-analysis by Murphy et al. (2009), who found that some classrooms were highly effective at promoting students' reading comprehension during class discussion. That is, many students began to develop the subject matter vocabulary by hearing other students in planned discussion. We can intentionally plan for surface level learning while also ensuring we don't stop there, waiting for a so-called perfect moment for deeper learning that never seems to come. We highlight planned classroom discussions when we focus on deep learning in Chapter 3, but students should certainly be talking with one another at the surface level of learning. The phases of learning should be viewed as dynamic and fluid guides as opposed to rigid rules implemented in a strict formula.

Surface Acquisition and Consolidation

Surface (and deep) learning consists of two subphases: acquisition and consolidation. Hattie (2012) argues that the pedagogical goal at the *acquisition* period is to help students gain initial understanding and an outline of the topic of study. The *consolidation* period leads to a second facet of learning, which is accomplished through practice testing and receiving feedback. We imagine this resonates with you at a fundamental level, in that it mirrors what we know about the science of learning. Students need to first acquire and then begin to consolidate the information. (The learning doesn't stop there, of course, but it's important to know where to begin.)

We'll use a nonacademic example of a universally relatable experience: learning to drive. It's likely that your introduction to driving took place at a safe distance from the vehicle. Whether in a driver education class (old school) or online (for our younger readers), the initial information you acquired concerned traffic laws and signage. Soon you were behind the wheel in a protected environment, and someone introduced you to steering, taught you how to set and check mirrors, and showed you how to operate the gearshift and brakes. All of this knowledge and skill was surface acquisition, in that you gained a general sense of the territory, and were able to summarize basic information and outline the steps of the driving process. At this time, telling you about defensive driving, how to anticipate other driver actions, or the mechanics of the clutch would be of limited use; you just want to know the basics.

But being able to correctly identify the brake and accelerator pedals is not driving.

You were now faced with having to consolidate the information. Figuring out how to operate the car while taking into account the traffic laws, signage, and changing conditions takes lots of time. You had lots of practice testing—low stakes—to refine your ability to apply the right amount of pressure to the pedals in order to regulate your speed.

And you got immediate feedback from the vehicle (remember that noise when you ground the gears?). Some of us may recall the terrified expression on the face of the well-meaning adult who sat in the passenger seat. We all know the reaction of parent instructors who rushed this early surface stage and could not understand why their child made such *obvious* mistakes—you need to overlearn many basic surface tasks before starting to get fancy! Consolidating freshly acquired knowledge and skills takes time, repetition, practice, rehearsal, and feedback. Looking back on our early driving careers, we know now we weren't ready to hit the highway under challenging road conditions.

We were only at the level of surface consolidation, not deep consolidation. We will explore instructional approaches to deep acquisition and deep consolidation of social studies learning in the next chapter.

Now let's put ourselves in the shoes of that well-meaning adult. If we had successful early driving experiences, it's attributable in large part to the skill of the person who was teaching us. He or she broke down complex skills into manageable parts, oversaw practice, scaffolded understanding, and provided feedback. Most of all, that person evaluated his or her impact by measuring your success. If you didn't perform a three-point turn correctly, that person knew the instruction needed to change. If he was skilled at this, he didn't say, "I've taught seven other people how to drive, and I am going to stick with this strategy even though I have evidence it isn't working with you." In other words, he didn't remain obstinately attached to a strategy at the expense of your learning. Instead, he adjusted his approach based on your achievement of desired results. Your learning was visible because of the way you were operating the car and because the driving teacher was paying attention and evaluating his impact on your learning. The practice of continually evaluating one's impact on learners is a key principle of visible learning (Hattie, 2009, 2012).

Acquisition of Social Studies Learning Made Visible

Teaching students to analyze the past and present, and then apply those concepts to present and future decision making is hard and complex work. We want our students to leverage their knowledge and skills in ways that allow them to gain new knowledge, critically analyze ideas, communicate conclusions, and collaborate with others in the democratic process. It would be wrongheaded to think that acquisition is something to be relegated to discrete fact accumulation. Kindergarten students can engage in both retention of key facts and complex thinking, provided they have had sufficient time and expert instruction on how to gain knowledge, critically analyze ideas, and so on. Each of these *begins* with the acquisition phase of instruction. In this section of the chapter, we will discuss social studies acquisition practices that yield effect sizes worthy of our time:

- Leveraging Prior Knowledge
- Vocabulary Instruction
- Teacher Modeling
- Wide Reading
- Note-Taking

Remember that at this early stage of learning, our pedagogical goal is for students to be able to stake out the territory by outlining the key landmarks of the unit of study.

Two important reminders are key to visible learning:

When the evidence suggests that learning has not occurred, the instruction needs to change (not the student!).

1. *The teacher clearly signals the learning intentions and success criteria* to ensure that students know what they are learning, why they are learning it, and how they will know they have learned it, and to maximize the opportunity for students to be involved in the learning.

2. *The teacher does not hold any instructional strategy in higher esteem than his or her students' learning.* Visible teaching is a continual evaluation of one's impact on students' learning. When the

evidence suggests that learning has not occurred, the instruction needs to change (not the student!).

Leveraging Prior Knowledge

So much of social studies learning can be described as disciplinary literacy—such as analyzing primary and secondary sources and making informed written or oral arguments. But literacy relies heavily on background knowledge. What a student already knows about a topic is an excellent predictor of how that child will perform in subsequent assessments of writing (Chesky & Hiebert, 1987), reading comprehension (McNamara & Kintsch, 1996), and word identification (Priebe, Keenan, & Miller, 2012). By extension, the effect size of a student's prior achievement—that is, his or her performance in learning—is significant. Although a teacher may have no influence over the knowledge a student has acquired in the past, the teacher has significant influence on how it will be leveraged. However, doing so requires

> EFFECT SIZE FOR
> INTEGRATING PRIOR
> KNOWLEDGE = 0.93

- knowing what the student already knows, and

- teaching with the intention to build on and extend the student's knowledge.

We have noted before that the knowledge students bring to the learning environment, and what we do (or do not do) with it, is "the missing piece of the comprehension puzzle" (Fisher & Frey, 2009, p. 1).

Possessing prior knowledge is one thing; knowing what to do with it is another.

What students already know about a topic may be jumbled, disorganized, and incomplete—and sometimes it can be plain wrong. Teachers can assess the prior knowledge of their students using tools such as anticipation guides (Tierney, Readance, & Dishner, 1995). Anticipation guides, such as the example in Figure 2.2, are designed to determine what students know, and are especially effective when they hone in on common misconceptions. Janice Hightower, an 11th-grade US history teacher, used the anticipation guide in Figure 2.2 to determine what her students knew, or believed they knew, about the US Constitution in advance of their study of the document.

ANTICIPATION GUIDE FOR US CONSTITUTION DOCUMENT ANALYSIS

Directions: Read each statement and answer true or false.

Before Reading	Statement	After Reading
	1. The document was ratified more than a decade after the colonies went to war with Great Britain.	
	2. It states that there must be a *separation of church and state*.	
	3. It guarantees everyone the right to vote.	
	4. It can be changed by passage of an amendment.	
	5. Public education is a guaranteed right.	

Explain why each statement is true or false.

Before Reading	After Reading
1.	1.
2.	2.
3.	3.
4.	4.
5.	5.

online resources ☜ Blank template available for download at **http://resources.corwin.com/VL-socialstudies**

Figure 2.2

"Every year I have a number of students who believe they know a lot about it because they have come into contact with it so many times. But there are some big misconceptions about what this document actually says," she explained. Rather than focus on isolated facts, she chose five statements that focused on broader understanding of the piece. "Only numbers 1 and 4 are true statements," she said. "I'm interested in their reasoning, and I ask them to complete this before, and then again after, we have discussed this. I want them to see how their thinking has shifted in light of their learning."

Vocabulary Instruction

If we want students to critically analyze historical and present documents, we need to be sure their reading comprehension is strong. Students have to understand what a text is saying before they analyze or evaluate it. Vocabulary knowledge is a strong predictor of reading comprehension (Baker, Simmons, & Kame'enui, 1998; Stahl & Fairbanks, 1986), and at the 0.67 effect size, strong vocabulary programs fall well into the zone of desired effects. Reading researcher Biemiller (2005), in his report on the choice and sequence of vocabulary words taught to young readers, reminds us that "[t]eaching vocabulary will not guarantee success in reading, just as learning to read words will not guarantee success in reading. However, lacking either adequate word identification skills or adequate vocabulary will ensure failure" (p. 223). However, vocabulary instruction, like other aspects of the curriculum, must be taught for depth and transfer. Unfortunately, too many children and adolescents experience vocabulary instruction as making passing acquaintances with a wide range of words. They know that many of the words won't be used again, and that next week there will be a new list to look at.

> EFFECT SIZE FOR VOCABULARY PROGRAMS = 0.63

In place of a passing view of words, vocabulary knowledge should be developed across five dimensions (Cronbach, 1942, cited in Graves, 1986):

- *Generalization* through definitional knowledge

- *Application* through correct usage

- *Breadth* through recall of words

- *Precision* through understanding examples and nonexamples

- *Availability* through use of vocabulary in discussion

We chose to address vocabulary instruction within the context of surface acquisition, knowing that teachers should never stop at simply exposing students to vocabulary. Learning a word requires not just exposure, but also repetition, contextualization, and authentic reasons to use the terminology in discussion, reading, and writing. We will return to the topic of vocabulary through the next few chapters, and we discuss deepening knowledge and fostering transfer of this unconstrained skill, while acknowledging that the starting point of vocabulary instruction is in knowing which words and phrases deserve to be taught. Too often, vocabulary selection is a hit-or-miss process, with some teachers identifying all the multisyllabic and rare words in a reading, while others cling to a list of words from the past. We suggest a decision-making process that considers the features of the word and the likelihood that the term or phrase will be acquired through other means, such as repetition or analysis. Only those that cannot be learned through these means are taught through direct instruction. Figure 2.3 presents the questions we pose, based on the work of Graves (2006), Nagy (1988), and Marzano and Pickering (2005).

A social studies supervisor for a large district shared this story: "In preparation for the annual benchmark assessments, a teacher and I gave his students a short text about immigration. We asked his Grade 9 students which words, if any, from the passage they found confusing. Over 30% of students listed the word 'immigration' as confusing. The teacher couldn't believe it! He had taught a whole unit on immigration just a few months prior."

This is a classic example of skimming too quickly over surface level learning, assuming students understand key terms. This story is not rare. Nearly all of us are guilty of plowing through units with important vocabulary words without giving sufficient time for students to develop their own understanding of the meaning of the words.

A DECISION-MAKING MODEL FOR SELECTING VOCABULARY FOR DIRECT INSTRUCTION

Condition	Questions to Ask
Representative	• Is the word representative of a family of words the student will need to know? • Is the word or phrase representative of a concept the student will need to know?
If yes, proceed to next section.	
Transportable	• Will the word or phrase be needed in discussion, reading, and/or writing tasks?
If yes, proceed to next section. Now determine how the word will be acquired.	
Frequency	• Does the word or phrase appear frequently in the text?
Contextual Analysis	• Does the word or phrase present an opportunity for the student to apply contextual analysis skills to resolve word meaning?
Structural Analysis	• Does the word or phrase present an opportunity for the student to apply structural analysis skills to resolve word meaning?
If the word appears frequently, and presents opportunities to resolve word meaning using contextual or structural analysis, the word probably does not need direct instruction. If the word is essential, and yet cannot be resolved through frequent use, contextual analysis, or structural analysis, the word or phrase should be introduced through direct instruction.	

Figure 2.3

Word and Concept Cards

Remember that we often need to situate social studies vocabulary within broader organizing ideas or concepts to help students make meaning of them and understand their significance. When you look at your standards of learning or outcomes, you may see a series of proper nouns (names of specific countries, documents, wars, presidents, organizations, significant events, geographic features, etc.). The next step is to ask what larger ideas these represent, and help students to determine the critical attributes of these broader concepts. Concepts help to organize factual information enabling easier retrieval of these proper nouns and specific details (Bruner, 1977; Donovan & Bransford, 2005).

SEE-IT MODEL

State, Elaborate, Exemplify, Illustrate, Talk (SEE-IT)
• State the idea clearly
• Elaborate on the idea (In other words . . . This is not to say . . . but rather . . .)
• Exemplify (For example . . . However, a nonexample would be . . . because . . .)
• Illustrate with a metaphor or image (It's like . . .)
• Talk with a partner and share your ideas

Source: Adapted from Stern et al., 2017; originally adapted from Paul & Elder, 2013.

[Download at resources.corwin.com/VL-socialstudies]

Figure 2.4

Next, plan learning experiences that require students to think about the meaning of these concepts in multiple ways. If we want students to remember key vocabulary words, we have to do more than define it for them and have them copy the definition. Middle school teacher Jeff Phillips uses a strategy called SEE-IT cards (Stern, Ferraro, & Mohnkern, 2017). This strategy asks students to explain and expand upon the meaning of words and concepts as they learn them. Figure 2.4 outlines the steps for this strategy.

Jeff explains, "My teaching team and I have the students create a series of cards with the concept written on one side and the State, Elaborate, Explain, Illustrate information on the other. Students collect these over the course of a few weeks as we introduce new concepts. We hole-punch them and use rings to keep them together.

These cards act as quick reminders of the concepts and help the students to quickly consider the words when trying to answer guiding questions or to better understand the relationships between the concepts themselves. Initially we began calling them Concept Cards but then another member of the team, Rena, mentioned that she liked the idea

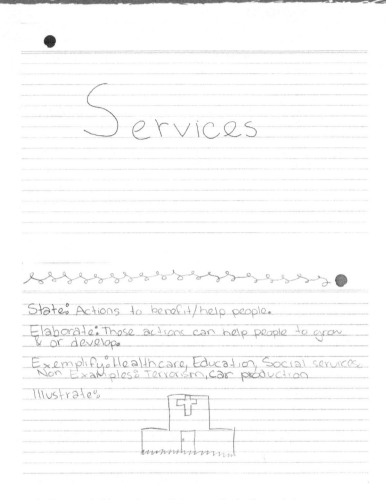

Services

State: Actions to benefit/help people.

Elaborate: Those actions can help people to grow or develop.

Exemplify: Healthcare, Education, Social services
Non Examples: Terrorism, car production

Illustrate:

Source: Student work provided by Hannah Eldon and Anna Christensen. Used with permission.

Figure 2.5

of having the students talk about their illustration after completing it so we quickly adopted the acronym SEE-IT (State, Elaborate, Exemplify, Illustrate, and Talk)."

An example of a student's completed card appears in Figure 2.5.

Concept Sorts

It is human nature that we actively seek out patterns to help us make sense of the world, and concept sorts make the most of this. Concept sorts require children to categorize similar examples using critical features that those examples share. In their seminal publication, the National Research Council (Donovan & Bransford, 2005) explained that the reason experts in any field remember more is that what beginners see as separate pieces of information, experts see as organized sets of ideas. They state that "using concepts to organize information stored in memory allows for much more effective retrieval and application" (p. 7).

A concept is simply an organizing idea, such as resources, built environment, natural environment, president, capital, democracy, and conflict. When we use concepts in social studies, students are better able to organize facts and dates within these more general categories. A strategy Julie often uses when teaching a new concept is to put the concept into Google images and see what comes up. Teachers can choose three to five images that illustrate the concept and ask students to discuss the critical attributes that the images share.

Grade 2 teacher Natalie Taylor used a similar method to teach the word *contribution* to her students. She used the word in three sentences to describe how teachers, doctors, and political leaders all make contributions. The students determined that the word means *to make a difference*. Asking students to figure out a word's meaning by looking at key examples helps them to better remember it in the future.

Grade 5 teacher Gina Thompson gave her students a series of pictures and asked them to sort them into two piles. There was a photo of a speed limit, a for sale sign in front of a house, a ballot box, a school, a newspaper, a church, and a few others. In small groups, students determined that one group of photos represented things you are *allowed to do* and things you *should do*. She used these to introduce the formal concepts of *rights* and *responsibilities*. Next, she gave labels to each of the pictures for students to match with the

Source: Gina Thompson's Class, Image courtesy of Kayla Duncan (2019). Used with permission.

Figure 2.6

pictures. She reported, "This activity was the highlight of my school year. Students debated about which items belonged in the rights category and which ones belonged in the responsibilities category even after the bell rang. I couldn't get them to leave my classroom. And the next day, they came in saying they had debated these ideas with their parents the evening before." This is the power of social studies learning done well. Figure 2.6 shows a picture from one of the groups in her classroom.

Teacher Modeling

How often have you wished you could see in the mind of someone who is an expert at what he or she does? Perhaps it is an athlete, or a musician, or a chess player. We mention these specific examples because they have been the subject of studies about the differences between experts and novices (Bransford, Brown, & Cocking, 2000). The expert in the classroom is often, but not always, the teacher. Like the athlete, musician, or chess player, he or she is able to notice, coordinate, and respond to subtle changes in systems. Moreover, many possess the ability to tap into their cognitive and metacognitive processes. In other words, not only do they know what to do, but they know why and how they are doing it. Unfortunately, all of this insight may stay locked away and out of sight from the ones who might otherwise benefit most.

Video 2.1
Modeling

*http://resources.corwin.com/
VL-socialstudies*

The act of teacher modeling and thinking aloud allows students to see inside the mind of the teacher to discover how decisions are made. Importantly, this includes possible strategies that are considered and discarded. It is useful for students to see that we rapidly move through several prospects before settling on an approach. This is particularly useful when students are acquiring disciplinary literacy skills. A think-aloud about how one analyzes a source is much more useful than quizzing students on whether or not they think a source is reliable without providing this important step.

After Grade 2 teacher Natalie Taylor facilitated a concept sort of the word *contribution*, she modeled her thinking of how she determined the contribution that Cleopatra had on the people in the kingdom of Egypt. She explains, "I read an article aloud and modeled what I was thinking as I read. I wrote down notes into a note-taking tool and told them how I recognized that these points were related to our word, 'contribution' so they understood how to do this on their own."

Social studies teachers can and should model important disciplinary processes such as how to analyze sources, place events in a greater context, determine the author's perspective, and recognize bias in primary and secondary source documents. A few tips to keep in mind include (Frey & Fisher, 2010)

- naming a strategy, a skill, or a task;
- stating the purpose of the strategy, the skill, or the task;
- using "I" statements to show your thinking;
- demonstrating how the strategy, the skill, or the task is used;
- alerting learners about errors to avoid;
- assessing the usefulness of the strategy or skill.

Wide Reading

Unlike the natural sciences, which tend to be more objective and straightforward, nearly all of social studies inevitably involves multiple perspectives and points of view on any given situation. A vital skill for democratic citizenship is the ability to sit with two or more different, even opposing, accounts of a situation and decide which is closest to the truth. It is essential, therefore, to provide students with multiple exposures to the same topic or situation.

We want to move students beyond thinking of primary and secondary sources as simply fact-based texts and develop their understanding that primary sources about the same event can present different points of view. At the transfer level, students need to compare texts but doing so requires that they understand each of the texts.

Students in social studies classes should have access to multiple resources such as magazines, books, videos, websites, and so on that contain informational texts. Many schools have subscriptions to World Book Online, World Book Kids, Time for Kids, Upfront Magazine, National Geographic Kids, and many more. When teachers incorporate multiple texts on the same topic, students expand their understanding.

Do you remember the big, pull-down maps above the chalkboard in nearly all classrooms when you were a child? Those are virtually nonexistent in today's digitally based classrooms. But so much of social studies requires students to picture the location of the situation or topic under study. Be sure to include maps at the start of every unit, even if they are digital, and ask students to refer to them often. Similarly, we can show students different maps of the same location that depict different data or even similar information depicted differently to illustrate various points of view about map depictions.

The importance of choice and volume cannot be overstated here: students who have more choices in what they read will read more (Guthrie & Wigfield, 2000). Children who read for more minutes each day are exposed to a higher volume of words, which in turn correlates to higher levels of achievement (Anderson, Wilson, & Fielding, 1988).

When we expose students to wide reading, they start to build the necessary patterns of thinking in the brain that are essential for moving to deeper social studies learning.

We recommend coordinating social studies instruction with other disciplines, particularly language arts and even science topics such as human-environment interaction. Language arts and social studies share many common disciplinary skills such as perspective-taking and analyzing informational texts. We can even coordinate topics in social studies with historical fiction such as using excerpts from Ken Follet's Century Trilogy (2010, 2012, 2014) for modern World History courses or *Invisible Man* (Ellison, 1952) or *Americanah* (Ngozi Adichie, 2013) for civics, sociology, or American studies courses. And we strongly encourage teaching students about diverse perspectives from texts. The organization *Doing Good Together* (www.doinggood together.org) has several book collections such as picture books and chapter books that teach citizenship, and issue-based collections such as the environment, human rights, and poverty. Another resource is the organization *We Need Diverse Books* (www.diversebooks.org), which includes an enormous compilation of links to sites that have books by and about diverse groups so that students can both see themselves in books and understand experiences different from their own.

Note-Taking

Another disciplinary literacy skill we often assume students already know how to do is note-taking. Note-taking is the practice of translating and transcribing key points during a lecture, while note-making (sometimes called text extraction) is done during reading. While the act of taking notes during class makes sense, especially when acquiring new information, its true value is more apparent when you consider how studying one's notes aids in strengthening knowledge, and organizing and transforming information in preparation for transfer of learning to new situations. We need to help students develop the sophistication involved in this skill throughout their schooling.

EFFECT SIZE FOR NOTE-TAKING = 0.51

You will recall from earlier in this chapter that the goals during the surface acquisition phase of instruction are for students to be able to take stock of the broad outlines of the area of study. We know they don't have the fine-grained details down yet, but it is useful to have a larger scheme in mind, however spotty, when examining the nuances. Summarization is useful for students acquiring new knowledge because they must build accurate and sturdy hierarchies of knowledge (Guthrie & Klauda, 2014). In other words, it contributes to their overall comprehension, and helps them to become aware of their level of understanding. When students construct written summaries of texts, discussions, and concepts, they engage in an immediate review process that allows them to notice where they are in their learning journey and receive timely and actionable feedback.

Teachers like Tyrell Washington integrate summary opportunities regularly into his Grade 6 class. "Ancient world history gets pretty complex for them," Mr. Washington said. "I've noticed that they get buried in the dates, names, and places we discuss, and miss out on the big picture. But I didn't really know how often that happened until I started having them write short summaries a couple of times each period."

Like many teachers, he had previously done this exclusively at the end of class—"a ticket out the door," he explained. "I definitely got good feedback that I could take action on the next day, but I got more concerned about early in the unit, when all the information is new." Mr. Washington started asking students to write short summaries of a few sentences throughout his early unit lessons so he could respond more quickly.

"I'll give you an example from yesterday," he said. "We're studying Pompeii right now, and when I had them summarize what we had discussed and read about, quite a few of them still thought the place was overrun by lava. That was their internal model for how volcanoes work, and they missed the point that it was the intense heat and gases that killed so many people," said the social studies teacher. "I had to fix that right away, and I could because they were writing these short summaries halfway through the lesson."

A common method for teaching secondary students about note-taking is the Cornell method (Pauk & Owens, 2010), originally designed by Walter Pauk when he was the director of the reading and study center at Cornell University. See Figure 2.7 for a template of the notes followed by an example of a student's notes from teacher Leah McGray's world history classroom. Using this method, students learn to divide their notes into three sections then use them to practice the "6 Rs":

1. *Record* the lecture notes in the main section of the note page.

2. *Reduce* the essential ideas by reviewing the notes within 24 hours and phrasing these ideas as questions.

3. *Recite* the information aloud by answering these questions while keeping the notes portion covered.

4. *Reflect* by asking oneself about how well the material is understood, and what clarifying questions should be asked of the teacher.

5. *Review* during subsequent short study sessions.

6. *Recapitulate* the main ideas by writing them in the Summary section.

FORMAT FOR CORNELL NOTES

Cues	Notes
For main ideas. Phrase as questions. Write within 24 hours after class.	Record lecture notes here during class. Use meaningful abbreviations and symbols. Leave space to add additional information.

Summary

Main ideas and major points are recorded here. These are written during later review sessions.

[Download template at resources.corwin.com/VL-socialstudies]

Figure 2.7

Consolidation of Social Studies Learning Made Visible

Surface learning of disciplinary skills and concepts is more than just introduction; students also need the time and space to begin to consolidate their new learning. It is through this early consolidation that they can begin to retrieve information and apply it in more sophisticated ways that will deepen their learning. However, the process of consolidation and recall of new information is surprising. Although it would be logical to assume that recall of new information right after it is taught would be higher than 24 hours later, it appears that the opposite is often the case (Henderson, Weighall, & Gaskell, 2013). The researchers found that initial word learning of elementary students was better a day later than it was immediately after they were taught, and that their recall was further strengthened when word meaning was taught. Time is also a factor in consolidation, and the opportunity to return to new learning again and again is further enhanced through rehearsal and memorization through spaced practice, receiving feedback, and collaborative learning with peers (Hattie, 2012). In this section, we will discuss high-yield strategies for consolidating surface level learning in social studies.

- Annotating Text
- Spaced Practice
- Receiving Feedback
- Collaborative Learning with Peers

Annotating Text

An essential part of social studies learning involves reading primary and secondary sources and taking note of multiple goals such as the main idea, point of view, and the reliability of a source while reading. A challenge that many beginning and struggling readers face when summarizing text is that they are less accurate in determining the key ideas presented. Winograd (1984) studied the summaries of good and poor eighth-grade readers and noted that the students who struggled more often identified phrases and sentences containing "rich visual details that perhaps captured their interest. In contrast, more fluent readers seemed to be defining importance more in terms of textual importance"

(p. 411). As texts become more complex, central ideas and key details are often scattered among several sentences, rather than definitively stated in a single sentence. Guided annotation of text, including underlining, circling, and making margin notes, can improve student understanding of new knowledge, and builds the capacity of students to better engage in study skills (study skills, including things like annotation, have an effect size of 0.63). It is important to state that teaching such skills in isolation of content (e.g., a study skills class) is not likely to deliver desired results.

"We look for sentences that have the main idea all the time," said third-grade teacher Sara Wilkes. "When I'm doing a shared reading with them, I put the reading on the document camera, and we read it the first time to get the flow. Then we go back through and start talking about the main idea."

Her students have their own copies of the reading to annotate, and Ms. Wilkes moves back and forth between modeling and thinking aloud about main ideas, questions about the text, and connections to other ideas and texts, and then guiding students to locate these on their own and in small groups.

"It depends on where I am in the learning process," she said. "If we're still acquiring new information, I'm going to model how I locate the main idea and the key details. As we go deeper, I start shifting this responsibility to them. My goal is that they're increasingly able to do this on their own, even when I don't ask."

Social studies curriculum specialist, Vince Bustamante has found success in providing a series of digital, document-based questions for the teachers he supports. Using Google forms, the resources follow a similar format, helping both teachers and students become more efficient at analyzing texts and annotating sources. The source is provided, along with a key analysis question, and then prompts such as these follow:

- What is the source saying, in your own words?
- Is there more than one perspective in the source? If so, what are they?
- Using evidence from the source, answer the key question.

When we teach students a structure or format for annotating texts, the daunting task of analyzing complex texts become easier. Figure 2.8

Eliza Riegert
World History
August 6, 2019

Topic: Mesopotamia

Cues	Notes
• Who is Hammurabi? • What were some of the advancements • What was the code of 282 laws	— Mesopotamian Advancements • invented the wheel & plow * • developed a number system based on 60 • use of arches, ramps • Writing system: cuneiform * — Mesopotamian Empires • Sargon of akkad created the first empire in Mesopotamia • hammurabi* led the babylonian empire ◦ known for his code of 282 laws,* "eye for an eye" • uniform throughout religion • government managed society • social & gender inequalities

Summary
Mesopotamia was under control by priests for many years. It then changed to emphasize dynastic rule. Created many advancements we use today.

Figure 2.8

provides a helpful method for students to annotate primary and secondary sources (Monte-Sano et al., 2014). Once students master the skill of analyzing documents, we can take scaffolds such as these away and let students develop their own systems that work best for them.

Rehearsal and Memorization Through Spaced Practice

Disciplinary learning—whether it be sourcing, contextualizing, or annotating—benefits from the same kinds of techniques used to master other complex skills. This means that students need to regularly have the occasion to rehearse what they have learned. We cannot overestimate the importance of this consolidation—in many senses, the purpose is to *overlearn* the surface knowing so that students can more readily access this information when they move to the deeper, comprehension, and inferential tasks.

EFFECT SIZE FOR SPACED VS. MASS PRACTICE = 0.65

As stated previously, social studies students need to mentally locate the place in the world and the place in time of the topic of study. Geographic and historical awareness provide needed context as students investigate a situation. We previously emphasized the importance of wide exposure to maps and introducing map skills, students should now rehearse and memorize key information in social studies. Asking students to memorize geographic locations, for example, important milestones in history, vocabulary in economics, etc., should usually happen in the consolidating phase of surface level learning.

History teacher Krista Ferraro often asks students to *best themselves* by providing blank maps or incomplete timelines. Using a timer, she makes it fun (and nonpunitive) to see how many locations or important events students can accurately place during two-minute sessions. Students then check their work and record their scores. She provides five additional minutes to study and asks the class if they think they can beat their own scores the next day.

When students are able to recall important locations or events automatically, it frees up brainpower to focus on more complex thinking. We can use time to ensure students can accurately define important concepts by matching them to either real or hypothetical scenarios. We like to call this a concept-scenario matching activity. Take a look at Figure 2.9 and consider how you might create something similar to allow students to practice matching concepts to real or hypothetical scenarios.

I READ TOOL FOR ANNOTATING DOCUMENTS

Identify the author's argument in response to the historical question.	Read each paragraph and ask about the author's main idea.	Examine the author's reliability. ★	Assess the influence of context. ➡	Determine the quality of the author's facts & examples. ▭
• Put a big box at the bottom and write the author's main argument. Author believes the colonists.	• Underline sentences that tell you the author's main idea OR • Write the main idea in three to four words next to each paragraph.	• Star information about the author, his/her purpose, type of document, audience, and occasion for writing AND • Judge: Write one reason to doubt the author and one reason to trust the author.	• Put arrows next to information about the context – dates of docs, location, & events. Make timeline AND • Judge: Given what else was going on at this time/place, write why the author's argument does/doesn't make sense.	• Put boxes around facts and examples the author uses to support his/her argument AND • Judge: Write why the author's facts and examples are/are not convincing

Source: Monte-Sano, C., Paz, S. D., & Felton, M. (2014)

[Download template at resources.corwin.com/VL-socialstudies]

Figure 2.9

Asking students to respond to questions during the consolidation phase of surface level learning gives us insight into their understanding, and—sometimes more importantly—their misunderstanding. Grade 9 teacher Doug Behse asks his students to write a question or statement with the concepts they are studying during this phase of the learning journey. In this case, the concepts were perspective, power, leadership, rights, change, beliefs, and conflicts. Take a look at the student response in Figure 2.10 and consider what it tells us about student understanding and misunderstanding.

CONCEPT-SCENARIO MATCHING

1. Globalization	A. The cost of producing goods is cheaper in China than in the United States.
2. Outsourcing	B. Europe's economy is in crisis, which negatively affects the US economy because we rely on Europe for goods.
3. Comparative advantage	C. Jobs like phone operators for most US companies are now based in India instead of the United States.
4. Economic interdependence	D. McDonald's was formed in the United States but now exists in almost every country.

Figure 2.10

Notice in the first statement, the student states that a leader has the *right* to do something, but in democratic governments, the government has *authority* and people have *rights*. It's an important distinction as, according to Enlightenment philosophy, people have inalienable rights that cannot be taken away, while the government has authority that it receives from the people. We can use spaced practice to catch common misconceptions as well as rehearse factual information and conceptual understanding.

Receiving Feedback

A repeating theme you will read throughout this book is on the power of feedback to shape students' thinking. Feedback from the teacher and peers can provide learners with the information they need to move incrementally toward success. Of course, not all feedback is useful and constructive. Wiggins (1998) writes about feedback conditions across four dimensions: it must be

1. *Timely*. The timing of the feedback is critical. During the surface acquisition phase, discussed earlier in this chapter, learners are getting initial exposure to new knowledge. Feedback may be premature, and reteaching may be more effective. But soon after surface-level acquisition learning, during the surface consolidation period, feedback is essential, because students are just now beginning to rehearse and practice.

Perspective, Power, Leadership, Rights, Change, Beliefs, Conflicts

/

The power that comes with leadership gives a leader the right to change society's perspective on their beliefs.

Figure 2.11

2. *Specific.* We've all been buried in an avalanche of feedback that exceeded our present level of knowledge. Nancy recalls getting an overwhelming amount of feedback from her driving teacher, and needless to say, it all ended in tears. Looking back, the feedback the driving teacher gave her was specific about what to do next, but it was too much at one time, and well beyond Nancy's ability to listen to, process, and execute. Although not what the instructor intended, she froze and shut down, rather than persisted.

3. *Understandable to the Learner.* Useful feedback needs to be aligned to the level of the learner's knowledge. Hattie (2012) calls this "just in time, just for me" feedback, further noting that "feedback is most powerful . . . when it is related to the student's degree of proficiency (from novice to apprentice)" (p. 102).

4. *Actionable.* Feedback that is withheld until the summative assignment has been submitted, and with no possibility of revising and resubmitting, is neither timely nor actionable. Feedback that is vague ("Good job!") is not specific—and further, not understandable or actionable—as the student speculates on what exactly made it *good.*

Collaborative Learning With Peers

EFFECT SIZE FOR COLLABORATIVE LEARNING = 0.34

After acquiring surface level learning, students consolidate their understanding in the presence of peers through productive group work

(Frey & Fisher, 2013). Purposeful discussion of complex texts during the surface consolidation phase is an excellent way to provide access to readings. For example, students engaged in small-group and whole-class discussions have the opportunity to clarify their collective thinking. However, these discussions need to be structured such that there is a shared investment in the outcomes, including individual as well as group accountability for the task.

A common and highly effective method for promoting group work is the jigsaw method. But—and this is key—we must be sure we do it correctly. Students should begin the group work portion in like-groups, all studying the same topic or portion of reading.

In this group, they work together to clarify their understanding and become experts on the topic. Then they move to mixed groups to teach the rest of their new group on their original topic or portion of reading. Finally, they return to their original groups and talk about how their topic or part fit in with the others. This final step allows students to move from surface to deep as they examine relationships and see the connections between the parts.

Grade 2 teacher Michelle DiMarzio used the jigsaw method for students to understand the culture of a chosen African country. Importantly, she previously used a concept sort using examples from American culture to help students understand the word *culture*. During this acquisition phase, students determined that culture is *the way people live in groups, their patterns of behavior.*

Michelle shares, "I explained that we were going to continue our exploration of the continent of Africa by researching the culture of four different countries. To help understand the purpose of the activities I asked them how they thought we could solve the problem of having a lot of information to learn (the culture of four countries!) and not a lot of time. Several students referred to a prior activity in which the class was grouped to work on different topics and suggested we do the same. Next, I asked, 'How are other people going to learn about your country?' Several students suggested that they tell the class about it.

Video 2.2
Having Successful Collaborative Conversations

http://resources.corwin.com/ VL-socialstudies

EFFECT SIZE
FOR JIGSAW
METHOD = 1.20

I then explained a way to do this is to jigsaw. My intention was for the students to understand the purpose for their learning was two-fold, for them and to be able to share with their classmates."

When Michelle took the time to explain the purpose of the jigsaw, the accountability increased and motivated students to be sure to solidify their understanding of the chosen country. Their classmates were relying on them alone to learn about the culture of this country, and she made sure they understood this before beginning the jigsaw.

She gave students a note-taking tool to help them organize their learning. They first researched their chosen country on their own, taking notes on the tool. Next, they met in the first *expert group* all studying the same country and she noticed some students filling in blanks or even correcting information they had recorded. Now they were ready to move to mixed groups, each studying one of the four different countries, to teach their peers about the culture of their chosen country. When they return to their expert groups, the students discuss the similarities and differences between the group they studied and the others they heard about.

Conclusion

A strong start sets the stage for meaningful learning and powerful impacts.

Teachers need to be mindful of the place their students are in the learning cycle. Surface learning sets the necessary foundation for the deepening knowledge and transfer that will come later. But there's the caveat: teaching for transfer must occur. Too often, learning ends at the surface level, as up to 90 percent of instructional time is devoted to conveying facts and procedures (Hattie, 2012). But the challenge is this: we can't overcorrect in the other direction, bypassing foundational knowledge in favor of critical and analytic thinking.

Students need and deserve to be introduced to new knowledge and skills thoughtfully and with a great deal of expertise on the part of the teacher. And teachers need to recognize the signs that it is time to move forward from the surface acquisition and surface consolidation period.

When the learning is visible, students and teachers are in sync. Teachers signal their students about what is being taught, why it is important, and how they will both gauge success. Teachers use feedback to help their students consolidate their initial learning, watching and listening carefully for indicators that learners are ready to move forward, or need more time and practice. That adds up to a strong start for deepening students' social studies learning.

DEEP LEARNING IN SOCIAL STUDIES

3

Democratic societies rely on high-quality social studies instruction, cultivating students who delve deeper into issues and problems that vex humankind. Current and historical issues are almost always more complex than many people realize, which contributes to their controversial nature. The ability to hang with a problem requires persistence and a certain amount of confidence in one's ability to eventually arrive at a solution. We could list any number of heroic figures here, but keep in mind that at one point they were children. What happened to them in and out of the classroom that might have contributed to their willingness and ability to go deeper?

Chances are very good that somewhere along the way, their intellect was sparked.

We'd like to think it was a teacher who had a hand in doing so—perhaps a teacher who saw something in these students they could not see in themselves. That teacher likely constructed learning experiences that were relevant and interesting to the learner. We're not talking about entertaining, but rather inspiring students to take ownership of their learning and to continue long after the bell rings or school year ends. Of course, each of these heroes had surface-level knowledge that they could use to further the students' learning.

Deep learning occurs as we begin to uncover the relationships between two or more concepts and monitor how those relationships strengthen and change as we encounter new situations or information. When we understand a topic deeply, we can see patterns and connections that we likely missed when we initiated our study in this area (Anderson & Krathwohl, 2001; Mehta & Fine, 2019). In this phase of learning, we can help students to both detect those patterns and monitor their understanding along the way.

As an example, let's take a look again at the classroom of teacher Krista Ferraro. This example will help you to visualize the strategies that follow. Ms. Ferraro believes her students are ready to use their surface knowledge to explore the intriguing relationship between freedom and oppression throughout history. Her students have already acquired and consolidated surface level knowledge of the concepts of democracy, freedom, equality, opportunity, economic prosperity, social stability, slavery, labor, and land, all brought to life through the time period of the US Civil War and Reconstruction. Please note that you can tailor the fact-rich context to your specific learning outcomes or curricular goals.

Ms. Ferraro invites students in by asking about the relationship among the concepts in this specific context. She asks, "How do we account for the development of both freedom and oppression in nineteenth-century America?" She explains that they will explore this overarching question for the remainder of the unit. Students begin by creating a flow map of what they consider to be the most significant events related to freedom and oppression from the American Revolution through Reconstruction. They partner up and compare their selected events with a classmate, discussing similarities and differences and explaining why they chose certain incidents over others. Knowing that learning is an ongoing process, students readily make changes to their flow maps based on their peer conversations. Nearly all groups discuss the paradox that, although the country was founded on the idea of freedom, slavery was infused in the formation of the nation from the beginning. Students know that these flow maps are going to serve as a planning tool for their upcoming essay on the overarching question about freedom and oppression.

Next, students read excerpts from an article titled "Liberty Is Land and Slaves: The Great Contradiction" by historian Seth Rockman (2005). Ms. Ferraro has them reread certain passages, marking the text for key phrases and ideas. She asks them questions such as "What 'contradiction' does Rockman describe? What makes this a 'paradox'?" At the end of a class discussion, the majority of students agree that this statement is the crux of Rockman's argument: "It was not a coincidence that some people in nineteenth century America had liberty while others did not; rather, some people's liberty depended on the denial of liberty to others" (p. 8).

This argument causes a bit of cognitive dissonance among many students. One student tilts her head and says, "I've never thought about US history in this way. I've always thought of freedom and slavery as opposites and assumed that Thomas Jefferson's famous phrase 'all men are created equal' was hypocritical because he held slaves. But some of these key points by Rockman about the intertwined nature of the enslavement of some people—the very opposite of freedom—and freedom for certain other people are hard to ignore." For social studies teachers, this is a coveted eureka moment. The revelation that the world is more complex than one previously thought is a hallmark of deeper social studies learning.

> EFFECT SIZE FOR CLASSROOM DISCUSSION = 0.82

Students instinctively begin to wonder if their previous assumptions about the US Civil War and Reconstruction time periods hold true. Ms. Ferraro anticipated this reaction and has another text ready for her students, a chapter about how textbooks deal with racism and the Reconstruction Era titled "Gone with the Wind: The Invisibility of Racism in American History Textbooks," by James Loewen (Loewen, Stefoff, & Loewen, 2019). This time, Ms. Ferraro asks students to explicitly monitor their thinking as they read and take notes on their responses to questions such as "What are your thoughts as you read? What evidence does he offer in support of his critique? Do you agree with his concerns?"

> EFFECT SIZE FOR QUESTIONING = 0.48

Students then join groups of four to begin a reading strategy called reciprocal teaching. They've experienced it before so they know what to

The revelation that the world is more complex than one previously thought is a hallmark of deeper social studies learning.

EXAMPLE INSTRUCTIONAL STRATEGIES OF DEEP LEARNING

Example Instructional Strategies	What It Looks Like in the Classroom
Graphic organizer	• Students create a flow map of the most significant events related to freedom and oppression in early America
Class discussion	• Students discuss similarities and differences in their flow maps and edit them
Close reading	• Students read and reread excerpts from articles that illustrate the concepts
Metacognitive strategies	• Students monitor their thinking through question prompts and explain how their thinking is evolving
Reciprocal teaching	• Students read a new text in small groups while pausing every few paragraphs to summarize, question, clarify, and predict what the text is saying

Figure 3.1

Video 3.1
Reciprocal Teaching

http://resources.corwin.com/VL-socialstudies

do. They read silently and pause every few paragraphs to orally summarize, question, clarify, and predict what the text will say next. At the end of class, Ms. Ferraro explains that students should reread the chapters from their textbook on these two time periods for homework, through the perspective of James Loewen, and to return prepared to discuss their thoughts the next day. One student remarked, "I can't believe I'm actually excited to go back and reread our textbook with a new perspective, to see if Loewen is right and to see if I missed something when I read it the first time." These students were equipped with the tools they needed to continue deepening their understanding of this momentous period in history as well as analyze the ways in which we construct historical accounts. However, it was Ms. Ferraro's structuring of the learning environment that ensured that they did. See Figure 3.1 for a chart outlining the strategies exemplified above.

Moving From Surface to Deep

The concept of surface and deep learning dates back to researchers such as Marton and Säljö (1976) and Biggs (1999). Each has described these constructs as internal to the learner, but under the influence of the teacher and the context. Surface learners are described as relying on memorization and are concerned about failure; therefore, they are risk-averse. Deep learners, on the other hand, seek to interact with content and ideas, and actively link concepts and knowledge across content. But Lublin (2003) states,

> One of the major concepts to emerge from this research was the idea that students can take different approaches to learning. These approaches are not stable traits in individuals, although some students will tend towards taking a deep approach while others will tend towards taking a surface approach (Biggs, 1999). Rather, it is suggested that good teaching can influence students to take a deep approach, while poor teaching in the widest sense can pressure students to take a surface approach. Biggs defines good teaching as the encouragement of a deep approach to learning. (p. 3)

In other words, the classroom environment can either encourage or discourage a learner from adopting a deep view of learning. A teacher who emphasizes (and assesses) surface learning will cultivate surface-level learners. On the other hand, teachers who encourage learners to plan, investigate, and elaborate on their learning will nurture deep learners. And the teacher who emphasizes a strategic mode will nurture students who learn when to be surface and when to be deep. Whatever you pay attention to is what your students will pay attention to. What you test is what your students will believe you value. As we described in the previous chapter, initial social studies learning is a necessary starting point as students begin to acquire and consolidate their surface-level knowledge. But if you turn too quickly to the next set of facts without giving students sufficient time and tools to go deeper, they will quickly learn that surface learning is what you value, and in turn, surface learning is all that you will get.

Whatever you pay attention to is what your students will pay attention to. What you test is what your students will believe you value.

It is at this point that the handwringing begins, and the talk of *covering the curriculum* and adhering to a pacing guide comes to the forefront. But if we truly stand behind the belief that teaching is about impacting

Video 3.2
Deeper Learning

http://resources.corwin.com/
VL-socialstudies

learning, rather than stuffing heads with facts, then we need to reexamine how the curriculum we are working with is constructed. In nearly every case, there is a spiral to the curriculum, and an expectation that students by the end of the year will be able to do more, in more knowledgeable ways, than they could at the beginning of the year. And when students are equipped to deepen their learning, the pace of learning quickens. Think of it this way: it needs to start slow in order to go fast.

Therefore, this chapter is about providing students with the tools they need to become deep learners. We focus on practices that have strong effect sizes—actions that ensure that students demonstrate at least a year's worth of learning. The previous chapter focused on initial acquisition and consolidation of knowledge. This one shifts to methods for not simply facilitating, but *activating* students' social studies learning in ways that allow them to become more independent. Deep learners are able to think metacognitively, take action, discuss ideas, and see errors as a necessary part of learning.

Hattie and Yates (2014) described this as System 2 learning, in contrast to System 1, or surface, learning:

> System 1 is fast and responds with immediacy; System 2 entails using time to "stop, look, listen, and focus" (Stanovich, 1999). More recently Daniel Kahneman (2011) wrote about the two systems he distinguished as "thinking slow" and "thinking fast." Slow thinking is System 2, which requires deep, challenging, and sometimes "hurting" thinking. Fast thinking is System 1, which rapidly calls on knowledge to be used in thinking slow. The more we make learning automatic (like learning the times tables) the easier is it for us to devote our cognitive resources to System 2 deeper tasks (such as using the times tables to problem solve). (p. 28)

The problem lies not with surface learning, per se, but rather with failing to move students into deeper learning. As we discussed in Chapter 2, we want students to be able to automatically pull up geographic locations and features of the world and key points in history in order to place a topic or event in context for further study. The next step is to move to deeper levels of social studies learning.

But how?

By equipping students with the tools and affording them the opportunity to do so. To us, transfer is the ultimate goal of learning, and we will explore this in more detail in the following chapter. But moving from surface level to transfer level requires valuable time spent in deep learning, where students recognize connections and relationships between ideas while monitoring the refinement of their understanding along the way. As Wineburg (2018) explains, "The mind demands pattern and form, which build up slowly and require repeated passes, with each pass going deeper and probing further" (p. 29). Students need to organize information to build patterns of thought, or schema in their minds. This is a fundamental distinction between novices and experts and one that can be explicitly cultivated with our learners (Bruner, 1977).

This chapter will focus on specific strategies used to help students organize schema, and the next chapter will focus on transfer of learning to novel contexts. But the tricky thing to keep in mind is that when we transfer our learning to a new situation, we deepen learning. We can think about applying the strategies of this chapter in multiple contexts that are highly similar from one situation to the next. And then in Chapter 4, we will learn more strategies for transferring learning to increasingly dissimilar contexts.

Learning Transfer Cycle (see Figure 3.2) describes the reciprocal relationship between abstract questions and specific contexts (Stern, Ferraro, & Mohnkern, 2017). Implementing the cycle provides students opportunities to practice applying their understanding to new situations and requires that they monitor their thinking as they organize and deepen their learning. As we'll see in the next chapter, we can increase the complexity and cognitive leap between novel situations. For now, it's important to use highly related contexts to build the necessary patterns of thought required for complex transfer to occur.

THE LEARNING TRANSFER CYCLE

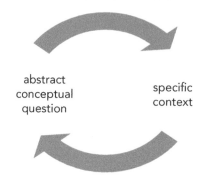

abstract
conceptual
question

specific
context

Source: Stern, Ferraro, & Mohnkern (2017).

Figure 3.2

The cycle usually goes something like this:

1. Pose a question about the relationship between or among two or more concepts, then study a particular fact-rich context that illuminates the answer to that question.

2. Students answer the question in light of the context and start to organize conceptual relationships, grounded in fact-rich detail. Then we repeat the process with another context.

We can think of specific contexts broadly as general learning experiences, even texts. Referencing our previous example, teacher Krista Ferraro posed the question *What is the relationship between freedom and oppression?* Students read "Liberty Is Land and Slaves" (Rockman, 2005) as the first context to help answer that question. Then they moved to another context or text, the chapter critiquing textbooks by James Loewen (Loewen, Stefoff, & Loewen, 2019) to further refine their understanding about the relationship between freedom and oppression.

As we saw with Ms. Ferraro, teachers can use specific instructional strategies along the journey of the Learning Transfer Cycle that further provide students with the necessary methods to deepen their learning. In this chapter, we will highlight some of the types of teaching strategies that will help provide students with these tools:

- Graphic Organizers and Concept Maps

- Class Discussions

- Close Reading

- Metacognitive Strategies

- Reciprocal Teaching

- Feedback to the Learner

Deep Acquisition and Deep Consolidation

As with surface learning, deep learning is divided into two periods: deep acquisition and deep consolidation. While the intention of surface learning is to expose students to and embed knowledge, the goal of deep learning is to both build larger schemas of organized understanding or patterns of thought about social studies content, and to increase self-regulation and self-talk. These two behaviors are critical for anyone moving toward greater expertise.

You might recall a learning experience you undertook in your own life that exemplifies these two behaviors. For example, Julie is a James Madison Constitutional Scholar, but this distinction was not achieved overnight. She remembers enrolling in a challenging law school course titled US Legal History where she had to put the knowledge and skills she possessed to use in authentic ways to show her what she was capable of doing. Although she previously completed extensive coursework in both political science and sociology, she was unfamiliar with the ways in which lawyers and law students study topics. She was used to investigating various groups that wielded power in society and analyzing the ways in which these entities affected different groups of people and society as a whole. Lawyers, it seems, zoom in on court cases and case law, tracing court decisions and organizing them into a coherent story. In order to keep up, Julie joined a study group, gained access to case law databases, and reviewed pertinent court cases before and after class and study group sessions. The self-regulation, strategic thinking, and self-talk she acquired in the process were useful when she had to wake early to look up cases, or forego attending a party with friends in order to review her notes.

Like other complex skills, students need opportunities to acquire and consolidate the use of these skills, in similar fashion to the acquisition and consolidation of knowledge discussed in the previous chapter. In the case of deep acquiring, students are learning how to plan, organize, elaborate, and reflect. They further consolidate through self-talk and self-questioning, both of which are necessary to becoming increasingly aware of their own metacognition.

EFFECT SIZE FOR SELF-VERBALIZATION AND SELF-QUESTIONING = 0.59

Social studies as disciplined learning goes part and parcel with the goals of deepening learning. Students need to talk about and listen to the ideas of others, especially those ideas that challenge their own current thinking. Students consolidate their conceptual understanding by writing. (We can't tell you how often we have figured out something through the act of writing.) Students doing deep learning link concepts, values, beliefs, and ideas through the acts of reading and viewing—but only if their teachers expect this as an outcome.

Classroom discussion can just as easily devolve into the familiar Initiate-Respond-Evaluate (Cazden, 1988) model of interrogation. Doug calls it "Guess what's in the teacher's brain":

Teacher: What is the capital of Canada?

Student: Toronto.

Teacher: Nope. Try again.

Likewise, social studies can be reduced to answering factual questions on a computer program or writing a summary of someone else's ideas, rather than a disciplined inquiry into past, present, or future situations. We get what we ask for, and when we fail to ask for deep learning, it is unlikely to emerge on its own.

Deep Acquisition of Social Studies Learning Made Visible

The pedagogical goal during the deep acquisition period is for students to assimilate knowledge, especially through integration with existing knowledge. This isn't merely an additive process. It's also subtractive, in the sense that new understanding may not jibe with previously held positions. The cognitive dissonance that results from being confronted by two contradictory ideas can be uncomfortable, and in that search for meaning, the learner has to make some decisions about how he or she will restore consistency. There's a higher degree of self-regulation that needs to take place, as students need to wrestle with ideas and concepts.

The ability to wrestle with competing or different points of view is essential for high-quality social studies instruction. "I tell my middle school students, 'I don't care what you think. I care that you *do* think and that you understand there are people who think differently than you,'" said Tiffany Mitchell Patterson, teacher and professor of social studies education. "Today's youth want to make an impact, but I make sure they understand that they need to know the historical context for whatever issue they are passionate about. And we have to help them embrace the nuance. We all have these multi-faceted identities and experiences that shape our world view. We have to help them understand points of view that are not their own."

> EFFECT SIZE FOR SELF-REGULATION = 0.52

Mitchell Patterson is signaling her expectation that her students will deepen their own learning. True social studies learning is messy work. Too often social studies lessons reduce learning to fact collection of key events or places without moving to deepen understanding of the significance and impact of those facts. We are reminded that knowledge doesn't ultimately count for much of anything if it doesn't spark inquiry and resolve problems. Wiggins (1989, p. 48) notes that students need to develop intellectual virtues including the following:

- Knowing how to listen to someone who knows something you don't know

- Perceiving which questions to ask to clarify an idea's meaning or value

- Being open and respectful enough to imagine that a new and strange idea is worth paying attention to

- Being inclined to ask questions about pat statements hiding assumptions or confusions

A critical difference between experienced and expert teachers lies in their ability to move students from surface to deep learning. John and his colleagues compared the practices and artifacts of teachers who had earned National Board Certification (NBC) with those of teachers who had applied for, but did not receive, this designation (Smith, Baker, Hattie, & Bond, 2008). The assignments were telling: 74 percent of the NBC teachers' work samples focused on deep learning, while only 29 percent of the non-NBC teachers' work samples evidenced deep student learning. In other words, the experienced but nonexpert teachers devoted far more attention to surface learning at the expense of deep understanding.

Of course, simply telling students that they will engage in inquiry, investigation, and problem solving isn't sufficient if they don't have the time and tools to do so. In order to assimilate knowledge during this deep acquisition period, students should be interacting with the curriculum and one another as they plan, organize, and elaborate on concepts. Much of this is fueled through concept mapping, discussions, and methods for conducting investigations. These are enacted in social studies through the disciplined literacies of reading, writing, speaking, and listening.

Grade 2 teacher Michelle DiMarzio reflected upon her experience of intentionally moving to deeper levels of learning with these strategies. "I found this way of teaching to be exciting. Students were much more able to grasp the concept of culture when given multiple ways to learn about it—whole class discussions were lively due to all students having opportunities to research and talk in groups. Asking students to teach one other was helpful for all of my students as they were able to 'coach' the others. At this young age, reciprocal teaching was a little tricky, but engagement was high and incorporating a whole-group discussion as a class was helpful before they completed their individual writing prompt."

Graphic Organizers and Concept Maps

Graphic organizers and concept mapping are visual representations of the relationships between and among ideas. This helps students both unravel and piece back together complex situations in social studies. Unfortunately, they are too often reduced to the level of worksheets, with the goal being to fill them out correctly, rather than to see one's thinking develop on paper or screen. It's transformation, not replication, that's key. Used well, concept maps and graphic organizers afford students the chance to take real ownership with texts and concepts because they equip them with a tool for succinct summarization and visualization.

> EFFECT SIZE FOR CONCEPT MAPPING = 0.64

Another key to using graphic organizers and concept maps well is to see it as an intermediate step to something else. In other words, what will students do with the graphic organizer once they've completed it? Most often, we use them to support extended writing and discussion of ideas. These are ultimately planning tools and are frequently used during the prewriting process as students begin to outline their ideas and develop an organizational structure to follow (Flanagan & Bouck, 2015).

As with so many other instructional strategies outlined in this book, timing plays an important role. Moore and Readence (1984) reviewed studies on the use of graphic organizers, noting that those that were completed and presented to students in advance of a reading had a relatively small effect (0.08). However, those that were constructed by students after reading text were much higher (0.57), and students processed and rehearsed information differently. More recently, Swanson et al. (2014) found that the use of graphic organizers with students with learning disabilities positively impacted their comprehension of social studies texts. Their meta-analysis examined several literacy instructional practices, advising that "educators should embrace instructional practices and materials that support the facilitation of activating *what was already learned*" (p. 179; emphasis added). In other words, the greater effect was found in aiding students to deepen their knowledge, rather than in acquiring initial knowledge.

Concept maps have a strong effect size, but as always, it's the story behind the numbers that really matters. Concept mapping is effective when it is used as a planning tool for something else. If its use is limited to filling it out and then setting it aside, it is no longer effective. The power of a concept map comes from the cognitive work it prompts as students lay out a schema of what they know. Their planning—for writing, research, investigation, or presentation—is what makes it so useful.

Grade 6 teacher Jeff Phillips uses graphic organizers to help students deeply explore a social issue of their choice. "Recently, students engaged in a book club around social issues. Students were able to select an issue that interested them and then read a book that explores that issue. They met weekly for three weeks to discuss how different texts dealt with the same issue. Then, students were asked to take their understanding of that social issue further by researching it and then creating a children's picture book aimed at students in Grades 2 and 3."

Mr. Phillips is using the graphic organizers to help students explore their topic in depth, but also as a planning step for creating an additional task—in this case, a picture book for younger students. Jeff explained, "To get started with the planning of their books, the students created a basic graphic organizer to gather as many ideas as possible about the social issue they chose to focus on. Then, students chose one idea and used a sequencing organizer to plot out the structure of the nonfiction text. The graphic organizers help students to get their ideas on paper and give them the space to be messy, make mistakes, and refine their thinking in a visual way."

Figure 3.3 shows an example of a flow map for sequencing events, which is one way for students to organize their social studies learning. In the deeper phase of learning, we want to be sure to use this to allow students to select the most important information to depict in the organizers. There should not be a *master key* organizer and students should not simply copy information into it. In the examples that follow, students chose from among many pieces of information or events from a time period, they did not to copy directly from the textbook or other source.

Grade 2 teacher Michelle DiMarzio uses graphic organizers to help her young learners organize their thinking. Students used an organizer to

FLOW MAP EXAMPLE OF STUDENT-SELECTED KEY EVENTS FOLLOWING THE CIVIL WAR

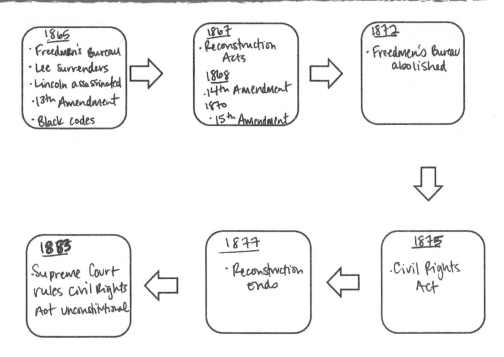

1865
· Freedmen's Bureau
· Lee Surrenders
· Lincoln assassinated
· 13th Amendment
· Black codes

1867
· Reconstruction Acts
1868
· 14th Amendment
1870
· 15th Amendment

1872
· Freedmen's Bureau abolished

1875
· Civil Rights Act

1877
· Reconstruction Ends

1883
Supreme Court rules Civil Rights Act unconstitutional

[Download blank template at resources.corwin.com/VL-socialstudies]

Figure 3.3

guide their research into the culture of an African nation. Ms. DiMarzio explains, "By allowing students to first research on their own, and then work in groups, they were given the chance to first find and record the information and then talk about it, and even add to their organizers if others had something else, or clarify mistakes. This allowed students to deepen their understanding of the elements of culture and specifically that of their chosen nation.

They all knew the next step would be to move to different groups to share a similarity and a difference about the cultures they've learned. They also knew that after this step, we would move to a whole class discussion."

MULTI-FLOW MAP EXAMPLE OF CAUSES AND EFFECTS OF POLLUTION

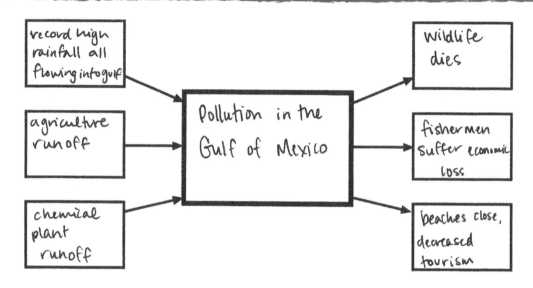

[Download blank template at resources.corwin.com/VL-socialstudies]

Figure 3.4

This teacher correctly uses concept maps and graphic organizers to help students organize their thinking in preparation for another task. Deep learning in social studies involves students organizing ideas into relationships. Figure 3.4 shows a multi-flow map for cause and effect while Figure 3.5 shows a double-bubble map for comparing and contrasting.

Class Discussion and Questioning

Free and open societies depend upon our ability to discuss complex issues and topics. Education researchers have advocated for the use of classroom discussion for promoting deeper learning for several decades. But there is a considerable gap between high quality discussion and

EFFECT SIZE
FOR CLASSROOM
DISCUSSION = 0.82

DOUBLE BUBBLE MAP EXAMPLES FOR COMPARING AND CONTRASTING

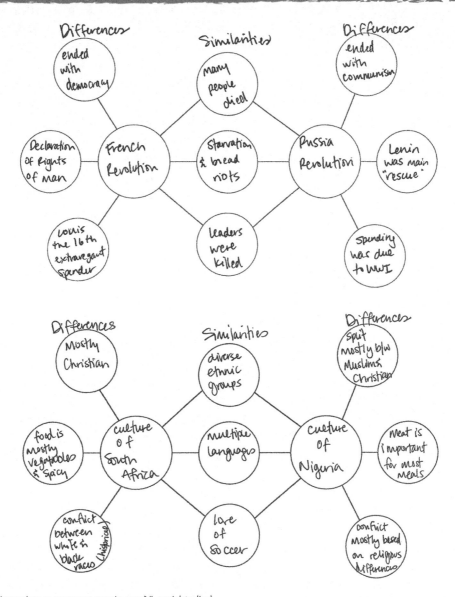

Differences
- ended with democracy
- Declaration of Rights of man
- Louis the 16th extravagant spender

French Revolution

Similarities
- many people died
- Starvation & bread riots
- leaders were killed

Russia Revolution

Differences
- ended with communism
- Lenin was main "rescue"
- Spending was due to WWI

Differences
- Mostly Christian
- food is mostly vegetables & spicy
- conflict between white & black races (historical)

Culture of South Africa

Similarities
- diverse ethnic groups
- multiple languages
- love of soccer

Culture of Nigeria

Differences
- split mostly b/w Muslims Christian
- Meat is important for most meals
- conflict mostly based on religious differences

[Download template at resources.corwin.com/VL-socialstudies]

Figure 3.5

EFFECT SIZE FOR
QUESTIONING = 0.48

Although there
is widespread
agreement that
discussion is vital
to comprehension
and critical
thinking, the
implementation is
severely lacking.

what teachers often refer to as classroom discussion (Larson, 1999). We need to be sure we are not confusing recitation level or basic recall questions with genuine discussion among students.

We've chosen to place discussion and questioning in the same section because we believe that effective teacher and student questioning fosters quality talk in the classroom. This is different from the Initiate-Respond-Evaluate method of recitation and interrogation, where the teacher asks the questions, evaluates the response given by the student, and then asks another question (Cazden, 1988). The IRE pattern encourages recitation of the correct answer, but fails to deepen student thinking beyond the surface. Although there is widespread agreement that discussion is vital to comprehension and critical thinking, the implementation is severely lacking. Nystrand's (2006) observations of middle and high school classes found that the average length of whole class discussions varied from 14 to 52 *seconds* per period—hardly enough time for anyone to deepen his or her knowledge.

The evidence suggests that the students who benefit most from classroom discussion are those who are struggling to comprehend text, although why is not clear. Could it be that discussion allows for students to coconstruct knowledge, in that the ideas introduced by one member spark understanding in another? Are classroom discussions effective because they heighten the level of student engagement with the topic? Is it the value in noticing that other people think differently than we do (Wilkinson & Nelson, 2013)?

But just because students are talking more doesn't mean that it automatically results in deeper learning. There are some quality indicators related to solid discussion (Fisher & Frey, 2014). Students need to know the rules of discussion, both in small groups and as a whole class, as well as procedures for doing both. One of the expectations for students in Grades 3–5 is that they learn how to yield and gain the floor. But to do so means that the teacher needs to redefine his or her role in the discussion. By this age, children have learned that they need to raise their hand and be called on before speaking. Yet this can result in stilted conversation, and the teacher becomes the air-traffic controller. There are certainly times when this is necessary, but we argue that true discussion occurs when students get to talk to one another without the teacher always being the intermediary.

Small-group discussion is also essential as students delve more deeply into the topics they are studying. These discussions are not directed by the teacher, but instead are regulated by the students themselves. Useful discussion should allow students to engage in argumentation as they justify their positions and listen to the reasoning of others (Almasi, 1994). We call it *disagreeing but not being disagreeable.*

Discussion is further strengthened when learners know how to mark the conversation, using statements that promote cohesion of ideas. These conversation markers include the following in Figure 3.6 (Michaels, O'Connor, Hall, & Resnick, 2010):

Teacher questioning frames these whole class and small-group discussions. The questions asked can limit thinking, as is the case when teachers ask narrow questions with only one response. On the other hand, teachers can invite further speculation by changing the nature of the question to prompt more discussion. The first are funneling questions, in that they intentionally send students down a cognitive path with a known end point. Funneling questions have their place, especially in the surface acquisition period. But deepening understanding through discussion requires a focusing question approach (Wood, 1998). Consider the likely responses that would follow the funneling examples, and compare your predictions to those that focus student thinking:

> Funneling: What was happening in the time period when this event took place?
>
> Focusing: How did the surrounding context impact how the event unfolded?
>
> Funneling: What is the meaning of the word *unalienable*?
>
> Focusing: Why do you believe the author chose the word *unalienable* in this passage?

We argue that true discussion occurs when students get to talk to one another without the teacher always being the intermediary.

SAMPLE CONVERSATION MARKERS FOR CLASSROOM DISCUSSION

"Can you tell us more about that?"

"Can you show me where you found that information?"

"I agree with _____ because _____ ." "That's a great point."

"I want to add on to what _____ just said."

Source: Michaels, O'Connor, Hall, & Resnick, 2010

online resources | Sample conversation markers available for download at **resources.corwin.com/VL-socialstudies**

Figure 3.6

When students are initially grappling with a complex piece of text, the questions teachers pose are frequently funneling questions. That's because students need a solid foundation of literal-level understanding about what's happening in the text. But after this initial phase of questioning, we want to deepen students' understanding through the type of focusing questions that get them to notice the structural and inferential dimensions of the reading. Figure 3.7 describes four phases of text-dependent questions (Fisher, Frey, Anderson, & Thayre, 2015):

These questioning phases are designed to systematically deepen a learner's understanding of a text, and discussion lies at the heart of close reading. We'll say more about the details of close reading in the next section but, for the moment, want to emphasize the role of text-dependent questions that focus, rather than funnel.

Grade 2 teacher Natalie Taylor conducted a class discussion on leaders of different countries. She explained, "I gave the students the conversation starters (from Figure 3.6) to use during the discussion. I held the students accountable by doing a checklist and seeing how often the students participated. The students elicited deep discussion by building on each other's points while describing how some of the leaders didn't contribute positively and how some of them did."

FOUR PHASES OF TEXT-DEPENDENT QUESTIONS

What does the text say? (Literal) How does the text work? (Structural)

What does the text mean? (Inferential)

What does the text inspire you to do? (Interpretive)

[Download at resources.corwin.com/VL-socialstudies]

Figure 3.7

Close Reading

The practice of close reading, an instructional technique for inspecting a brief passage of text to determine its inferential meaning, is not a new one. Its history dates back to the 1920s, when New Criticism was on the rise as a means for interpreting texts at the word and sentence levels, as well as the entire passage (Richards, 1929). Close reading for many decades was the domain of college professors and advanced high school English teachers, and the works analyzed were primarily literary texts and poems. What is new about close reading is the application of many of these ideas in elementary and middle school classrooms (Fisher & Frey, 2012, 2014). This instructional routine combines several of the strategies profiled in this book:

- Students engage in repeated reading of a short passage to build fluency and deepen understanding.

- Students annotate text to mark their thinking.

- The teacher guides discussion and analysis through questioning.

- Students engage in extended discussion and analysis with their teacher.

Close reading varies according to developmental factors related to reading.

Emergent and beginning readers in the primary grades are read to, rather than reading independently. This is because the texts used during close reading are aligned more closely to their listening comprehension, rather than their ability to decode. The gap between children's listening and reading comprehension is substantial, and doesn't close until the end of middle school (Stricht & James, 1984). Close reading in primary is a time when the unconstrained skills of vocabulary and comprehension are foregrounded and decoding instruction takes a backseat.

As students move to Grade 3 and beyond, they assume responsibility of performing the initial reading on their own. Many have worried that this will place struggling readers in harm's way, but keep in mind that in close reading, students are reading and discussing the text many times. It's a form of slow reading, where the end game is not about volume but rather about depth of understanding. The teacher pauses frequently to ask text-dependent questions that cause readers to look back into the text (and thus reread). These are focusing rather than funneling questions and move from literal to structural and inferential levels of analysis. Because close reading is cognitively demanding, lessons are often extended over two or three sessions.

Kindergarten teacher Josué Paredes used the text *The Day the Crayons Quit* (Daywalt, 2013) to further explore the idea of persuasive writing. Even though this is a fiction book, it is a great example for students of all ages to explore claims, reasoning, and evidence in text. For those of you who haven't yet had the pleasure of reading this text, the story concerns a group of crayons who feel they have been treated unfairly and decide to go on strike. Each has written a letter to Duncan, the young boy who owns them. For example, purple crayon doesn't like the fact that Duncan uses him carelessly and colors outside the lines, and peach crayon won't come out of the box because Duncan has peeled off his wrapper.

After completing all of the steps of close reading, Mr. Paredes asked his students what this text inspired them to do. The majority of students chose to write about the book. But others selected different routes. Several children wanted to find out if the author wrote any other books, and visited his home page (with help from the teacher). Two boys were intrigued about the dispute yellow crayon and orange crayon got into regarding which was the proper color of the sun. The boys searched Google Images and saved images to sort into either orange or yellow. And one enterprising student chose to write her own set of letters, this time from her shoes. In her letters, some never got worn, others had to work on holidays, and a pair of flip-flops didn't like getting wet all the time.

Our point in telling you about this—students need teachers who give them the time, opportunities, and tools to deepen their knowledge. Mr. Paredes understands that if students are going to deepen their knowledge, he needs to plan for it. Many of these events involve investigation, writing, and performance. As they move into deep consolidation, they benefit from approaches that foster metacognition, self-talk, and the ability to examine texts outside the direct guidance of the teacher.

Social studies specialist Vince Bustamante works with teachers to increase students' abilities to conduct primary and secondary source analysis through close reading of short texts. Using digital protocols for short texts, including political cartoons, students first read and answer comprehension and inferential questions about the text.

Several of the questions ask students to cite specific evidence from the text to support their inferences. The responses to these questions are often explored further in class, allowing students to stick with a short piece of text for an extended period of time, sometimes an entire class period. This process improves students' abilities to take time with texts to deepen meaning.

> Students need teachers who give them the time, opportunities, and tools to deepen their knowledge.

Deep Consolidation of Social Studies Learning Made Visible

As students deepen their knowledge, they also need the time and tools to consolidate their deep learning. In this period, students are conducting investigations, reading additional materials, and working with peers to make sense of complex topics. They depend on metacognitive thinking and self-regulation as they progress toward this increasingly self-directed learning.

Metacognition is the ability to think about and reflect on one's learning (Flavell, 1979). This is where students are taught to be strategic in their planning, thinking, and learning. The process is both a learned one, as students build the habit of reflective thinking, and a developmental one, as they progress toward more abstract thinking. A comparison of the discussions held with a child and an adolescent certainly makes this apparent. Although a youngster has fewer tools (language, cognition) to explain her motives behind a transgression, a teen is going to be able to do so, even if she's not going to tell you. The ability to think more metacognitively begins around age 3 and develops into adulthood (Kuhn, 2000); it is further enhanced through strategies that build habits of reflection and by feedback that illuminates when strategies work and when they do not.

Video 3.3
Helping Students
Notice What They Do
and Do Not Know

*http://resources.corwin.com/
VL-socialstudies*

The conversations and discussions adults have with children can foster or inhibit thinking. For example, asking students, "What are you learning?" rather than "What are you doing?" gets them to attend to the purpose of the task at hand, rather than the activity itself. Asking students to "tell me what you understand so far" builds the expectation that they should be monitoring their learning. This last one is of particular value at the deep consolidation phase as it sets up the kind of student questioning you need to assess your own impact and make further instructional decisions. It's almost impossible to formulate a question about something you know nothing about; that isn't the case with students in this learning period. They know quite a bit, and can craft their next questions to you based on what they currently understand. Even more so, students should pose questions for themselves. Self-questioning plays an important role in monitoring one's comprehension (e.g., Johnson & Keier, 2011). A student who monitors her comprehension of the topic is also going to recognize when she has lost the thread of meaning.

While studying the culture of different nations, Grade 2 teacher Michelle DiMarzio wanted students to reflect on why learning about different cultures was important. "I asked students to respond to the following journal prompt, 'Why is it important to learn about different cultures?' I was pleased to see a vast majority of student responses indicated an emerging understanding of the importance of culture. Responses primarily focused on the usefulness of learning about other cultures in respect to traveling, having visitors, or meeting new people. A few students wrote about the need to be able to communicate, know the rules, or otherwise fit in with a new culture.

Several students included being respectful as a reason. I think the responses were strong because we intentionally moved through the phases of acquiring and consolidating surface learning about the word 'culture' and then continued with different strategies to acquire deeper levels of learning."

In the next section, we will discuss the value of strategy instruction to foster metacognition, self-questioning, and self-regulation. Students moving into deep consolidation are increasingly driving their own learning, and these thinking practices keep them moving forward. We don't mean to suggest that students are working independently, with little guidance from the teacher. Practices that foster such application include reciprocal teaching because it requires students to mobilize specific behaviors while engaging with complex topics as well as their peers. All the while, the teacher is providing feedback that models the kind of self-talk we want our students to be able to furnish for themselves. The deeper learning phase is a critical time for students to apply these approaches to their learning.

Metacognitive Strategies

Metacognitive awareness is vital to the learning process, and specifically when social studies students are doing the important disciplinary literacy work of reading and writing. Palincsar (2013) describes metacognitive awareness as consisting of three parts:

> EFFECT SIZE FOR METACOGNITIVE STRATEGIES = 0.55

1. Knowledge about our learning selves

2. An understanding of what the task demands and necessary strategies to complete them

3. The means to monitor learning and self-regulate

In other words, it describes our ability to observe our own thinking. Many teachers want their students to *think historically* or like an economist, geographer, political scientist, etc. But students need guidance in how to become more metacognitively aware. A collection of approaches, outlined in the pages that follow, is designed to teach students how to plan tasks, monitor comprehension, and evaluate their progress.

Self-Questioning

As a person encounters a new situation or topic, he or she is monitoring comprehension. This is not a fully conscious realization, but rather one that runs just under the narrative he or she is taking in. This skill is important for examining primary and secondary sources and particularly important in an era of questionable sources and information found on the internet. You have hopefully gone through this process yourself when coming across a news story headline or statistic. As you read or listen to the story, you are comparing it with your existing knowledge, asking yourself if you are familiar with the source, and wondering where you might find additional information. If something occurs to disrupt your understanding of these elements, you will probably either go back to reread, or pause the video to ask the person next to you, "What just happened?" Running in the background is a well-attuned method of self-questioning, as you continually ask yourself, "Does this make sense?" and if it doesn't, "What do I need to do to regain understanding?"

Humans are pattern-seekers and meaning-makers, and we continually strive to make sense of what is happening around us. When it comes to reading or watching online sources, there exists an innate need to make sense of the source. But students also need to be taught how to monitor their comprehension, and what to do when it breaks down. This is accomplished through two approaches:

1. Provide questions students can use as they query their understanding.

2. Teach students to pause periodically throughout a text to generate their own questions.

1. Provide Questions

Furnishing predetermined questions during the deep consolidation phase is useful as it reminds students about the metacognitive practices they need to propel their learning and monitor comprehension. It is common for students who are deep into a unit of study to engage in investigation and research. But the advent of online sources has introduced other considerations that teachers of earlier generations did not face. The internet is an excellent source for digital material, but it is also fraught with problems that can derail student projects. Chief among them are issues of credibility and accuracy of information. Teachers aren't able to curate source materials as they once did, and now must equip students with the ability to question both primary and secondary sources.

The Stanford History Education Group has conducted extensive research in this area of online reasoning. The vast majority of middle school students in the United States are unable to distinguish between the reliability of an online news story and an online advertisement (Donald, 2016). This group of researchers created resources to help students evaluate online sources. They encourage the use of three questions when encountering a source online (Civic Online Reasoning, Stanford History Education Group):

- Who's behind the information?
- What's the evidence?
- What do other sources say?

Another tool we can use with students is a website evaluation tool, listed in Figure 3.8. These tools are used to help students become familiar with the types of questions that we want to eventually become automatic and intuitive when they encounter new information. These tools serve as starting points before we help students to ask their own questions.

2. Teach Students to Ask Their Own Questions

A second method for fostering self-questioning is by creating points when they compose their own questions. This approach is particularly

WEBSITE EVALUATION TOOL

URL: _____

1. Title of website: _____

2. What is the main purpose of the website? _____

   Is it selling something?   Does it describe a service?   Is it an educational site?

3. Who created the website?

   Is there a contact name? Is it a private company? Is it a school? Is it a government agency? Is there an "about us" section?

4. How current is the website? (When was it last updated?) _____

5. Are links available to other sites? (Try some of them to make sure they work.) _____

   _____

6. Are there references or citations? If yes, what are they? _____

7. What new information did you learn from this website? _____

   _____

8. What information is missing? _____

   _____

Source: Fisher, D., Frey, N., & Gonzalez, A. (2010). *Literacy 2.0: Reading and writing in the 21st century.* Bloomington, IN: Solution Tree (p. 44). Used with permission.

[Download template at resources.corwin.com/VL-socialstudies]

Figure 3.8

useful as students read longer pieces of informational texts. Many children adopt a naïve assumption that people read long passages without interruption, and then process all the information at once. Teaching them how to break a text into more manageable chunks so they can use self-generated questions will equip readers with strategies for maintaining understanding.

Grade 5 teacher Joyce Gomez uses a method described by Berkeley, Marshak, Mastropieri, and Scruggs (2011) to build the habit of teaching

SELF-QUESTIONING INSTRUCTIONS

Directions: Before reading, write down a question you expect to be answered in each section. At the end of each section, see if you can answer your question. If you can't, use one or more of these strategies to help yourself.

1. Reread the passage with your question in mind.
2. Check for unknown vocabulary (look inside and outside the word or phrase).
3. Check graphs, diagrams, or photographs that are in the section.
4. Write your question to ask me about it.

[Download at resources.corwin.com/VL-socialstudies]

Figure 3.9

her students to engage in self-questioning when working with informational texts. She uses headings and subheadings in articles and textbooks as stopping points for students to ask themselves questions.

"When we first began doing this at the beginning of the school year, I did lots of modeling, as you can imagine," she said. "I taught them about why self-questioning is important and made note pages for them like this one to structure the process," she continued, displaying the sheet found in Figure 3.9. "As we've progressed, I have faded out the note pages and shifted them to writing questions in their journals. I leave it to them to chunk the text for themselves, because not everything we read has headings and subheadings."

Ms. Gomez speaks to individual students to check in with them about their self- questioning. "I ask them to answer a question they've written. If they can, I give them feedback about the use of this strategy. If they can't, I ask them about other strategies they can use to regain understanding."

Reciprocal Teaching

The emphasis in reciprocal teaching is on deploying comprehension strategies to make meaning, engaging in self-questioning, and chunking

RECIPROCAL TEACHING STRATEGIES

- Summarizing each passage to extract key information and central themes

- Questioning at the literal, structural, and/or inferential levels about the passage

- Clarifying information and ideas through discussion and checking in with peers

- Predicting the content of the next passage, given what the author has explained thus far

 Instructions available for download at **resources.corwin.com/VL-socialstudies**

Figure 3.10

texts into smaller passages. All of this is done in the company of a small group of peers, who work together to coconstruct meaning from text (Palincsar & Brown, 1984). The evidence of reciprocal teaching is broad: Palincsar (2013) notes that other researchers have found it to be effective with students with disabilities, English learners, and bilingual students.

Although reciprocal teaching can be used in service of students acquiring a surface level of knowledge, the expression of so many features necessary for deepening learning made it a good candidate for this chapter.

Reciprocal teaching (RT) is a structured reading routine enacted by four students who are working through a piece of text. Figure 3.10 shows how RT discussions are composed of four strategies, which are systematically introduced and taught.

The teacher segments the text into smaller chunks, and students are taught to pause after reading each segment to discuss its content using these four strategies.

Because RT enlists so many complex cognitive behaviors, teachers commonly introduce it across multiple lessons, as each comprehension strategy is practiced and then paired with subsequent strategies until students are adept at doing all four. In the early stages when students are still learning about RT, they are typically assigned these as formal roles (summarizer, clarifier, and so on). But as Palincsar (2013) notes, the larger goal is that students deploy these strategies "opportunistically" (p. 370). Therefore, formal roles and structured dialogues give way to more organic discussions about complex text.

Feedback to the Learner

The metacognitive and self-regulatory skills of students are strengthened through feedback from the teacher. When the feedback is delivered such that it is timely, specific, understandable, and actionable, students assimilate the language used by the teacher into their own self-talk. What we say to children, as well as how we say it, contributes to their identity and sense of agency, as well as success. The messages that students receive externally become the messages they give themselves. We're speaking not strictly of praise, but rather of making sure that we not only commend learners when, and for what, they are doing well, but also label their actions for them. When a student needs direction, our feedback should assist her in identifying the actions she needs to take in order to get back on the path. Saying to a learner, "What can you do next to find that answer?" sends an underlying message that she has agency and can take steps. In contrast, telling a learner, "The answer is on page 37," without giving her an opportunity to resolve what's blocking her, tells her that you don't believe she is capable of doing so. Students shouldn't be reduced to tears in trying to move forward—we don't want to withhold information from students indefinitely—but we do want them to develop the kind of self-talk they need to persist when things get difficult, and to bounce back when confronted with failure.

> EFFECT SIZE FOR FEEDBACK = 0.66

It's important to say that we are not enamored with failure. No one likes to strive toward something only to repeatedly fall short of the goal. Having said that, small failures are a part of the learning process, and can actually lead to a more attenuated understanding of why something didn't work the first time, so as not to repeat it again. It's not the failure in isolation that we're talking about, but rather the pairing of a small failure followed by a small success.

Effective teachers look for opportunities to give feedback to students by playing back what occurred. Saying to a student, "I can see you had trouble with this part of the assignment, but then you solved it. What did you do that led to this success?" alerts him to think reflectively about the strategic thinking and action he took to get himself over a hurdle. In doing so, we give him the internal scripts he needs to become an increasingly self-directed learner.

It is equally important that we not dilute feedback with praise. Dweck (2006) has written extensively on the damage praise about the individual can do in reinforcing a fixed mindset rather than a growth mindset. Students with a fixed mindset have been conditioned to believe that innate qualities such as intelligence and talent are the keys to success, and they discount the role of effort or their own agency. Although we don't mean to, too often we communicate our own beliefs in a fixed mindset when we tell students, "You're so good at reading primary and secondary sources!" instead of saying, "Your source analysis has really improved this quarter. I've noticed how much more time you're spending annotating and asking yourself questions about what you are reading. Look at the difference in your scores since the last quarter." Highlighting progress further builds a learner's sense of agency as he sees the relationship between his success and his actions.

Hattie (2012, p. 116) speaks of three internal questions that drive learners:

- Where am I going? What are my goals?

- How am I going there? What progress is being made toward the goal?

- Where to next? What activities need to be undertaken next to make better progress?

The feedback we give students at any point in their learning falls into four levels:

Feedback About the Task: How well has the task been performed; is it correct or incorrect? For example, "Your goal was to list all of the reasons why this event occurred so you can organize your essay, but the

> What we say to children, as well as how we say it, contributes to their identity and sense of agency, as well as success. The messages that students receive externally become the messages they give themselves.

second point is unclear. You need to change the wording so that your argument is stated using an active voice, rather than a passive one."

Feedback About the Process: What are the strategies needed to perform the task; are there alternative strategies that can be used? For instance, "I can see that you're not sure what categories you want to use for your concept word sort. What is another way you could solve the problem?"

Self-Regulatory Feedback: What is the conditional knowledge and understanding needed to know what you're doing (self-monitoring, directing the processes and tasks)? For example, "When you got frustrated with your group, you moved your chair back and took a breather. Then you rejoined them a minute or two later, and your group completed the task. Why did that work for you? How were you different after you rejoined them?"

Feedback About Self: Personal evaluation and affect about the learning. For example, "Excellent job! You are such a talented writer."

The first two levels, task and process, are more commonly used in classrooms, and we witness teachers using these on a frequent basis. The fourth level—feedback about self—is unfortunately used too often by well-meaning teachers. Although meant to bolster self-esteem, it appears to have a zero to negative impact on learning, especially in discouraging students from engaging in any further revision of their work (Hyland & Hyland, 2006). We want students to think positively about themselves, and praise is a tool that can contribute to positive teacher–student relationships. The message should not be interpreted as *do not give praise*; instead, the message is to separate the praise from feedback about the task, and the learning. It's important that adults don't withhold their unconditional positive regard for students, but praise that masquerades as feedback can undermine efforts to motivate and encourage.

But it is this third level of feedback—self-regulatory feedback—that plays such a prominent role during deep consolidation. Think about the instructional approaches we have profiled in this section. All of these methods offer critical opportunities for teachers to dialogue with students as they delve into increasingly self-directed learning.

In Ben Watson's economics class, students are analyzing the ways in which incentives to encourage alternative energy solutions influence what is produced and distributed in national and international markets. One of his students is having difficulty with considering multiple points of view on this issue.

Mr. Watson:	Let's take a look at your graphic organizers that show the positive and negative outcomes of different forms of incentives to encourage alternative energy. It seems you have found many benefits to incentives but have not been able to come up with many potential negative consequences. Tell me what you were thinking when you completed the organizers.
Hannah:	Well, I just don't see any negative consequences to incentives because if we don't change, we will continue to have catastrophic harm to our planet and societies, triggering global migration and millions of dollars in damage due to natural disasters such as flooding and drought.
Mr. Watson:	Mr. Watson: It seems that you are passionate about this issue, which is admirable. Do you remember what it means to think like an economist?
Hannah:	Yes, I remember. They have to put their own personal views and interests aside for a moment while they seek to analyze different economic policies. When I was doing a close reading with my group about the potential negative economic consequences of moving away from fossil fuels, I did start to see what the author was saying. Perhaps I can read that article again and complete the other parts of my graphic organizer.
Mr. Watson:	That's a great idea. At what points in the article did you begin to notice the complexities of this issue?
Hannah:	(pulls out the article) It was here when he began to predict the ways in which economies rely on the revenue generated from fossil fuels. I think I can find more information to be able to consider viewpoints that are different from my own.

Mr. Watson: That is very mature of you to be able to temporarily suspend your own points of view to analyze the situation more carefully. Let's talk tomorrow to see where you are with this.

This conversation illustrates the power of helping students to do their own thinking and reflecting about their learning journey. Mr. Watson did not tell his student what to do next, but instead prompted her to think about how she might improve her approach to her analysis, while keeping the conversation warm and encouraging. To be sure, the discussion took a few minutes to conduct. But the time is well worth it, and is critical as students move from deepening their learning to moving into transfer. Our efforts to equip students with the tools, strategies, and scripts for talking to themselves make moving to transfer, which is the subject of the next chapter, possible.

Conclusion

In order for students to deepen their knowledge, they need to have their learning made visible to them. It's how they can take action on what happens next. The language and behaviors we use with them assist them in understanding who they are as learners, what the task demands are, what strategies they can leverage to resolve problems, and how they can persist when things are difficult. Embedded within these is resiliency.

Learners who are resilient can come back from failures and incorporate challenges into their growing sense of who they are. Consider anything you've learned and that you value as an accomplishment. Without a doubt, you faced challenges, and sometimes some failures, as you completed that journey. Now consider who guided you along the way.

Chances are just as good that someone helped you gain the tools and strategies to move forward, using language and behaviors that you took to heart. Teaching requires lots of heart, along with an unflagging belief in the ability of your students to achieve success. Don't be afraid to tell them, and show them, your confidence in them.

> Learners who are resilient can come back from failures and incorporate challenges into their growing sense of who they are.

TEACHING FOR TRANSFER IN SOCIAL STUDIES

4

What do we do when we come across a new situation in the news or even in history that we previously had not known? Of course, we take the time to get to know the surface level details of that situation and we connect it to our related prior knowledge.

We draw on our associated factual knowledge using the relative attributes of organizing concepts—such as power, freedom, leadership, and resources. And we use our conceptual organization—the relationships between and among concepts—that has been built, strengthened, and deepened with each new situation we previously encountered. We also ask ourselves where our prior understanding holds true, and where we need to adjust, expand, or even change our thinking based on this new situation.

When Julie was living in Bogota, Colombia, the front cover of *Businessweek* magazine caught her attention. The headline read, "How to Hack an Election" (Robertson, Riley, & Willis, 2016) and featured a man named Andrés Sepúlvida. This man was serving time in a prison just a few miles down the street from the school where Julie worked, convicted of interfering in many elections around Latin America. The article appeared in 2016, when the United States was in the midst of a national election season and the United Kingdom was set to vote on whether or not it would leave the European Union. Intrigued, she sat down to read the article.

Although she was unfamiliar with most of the specific information in the article, Julie had enough background knowledge and conceptual organization about other elections as well as the use of technology—such as Twitter bots—to be able to understand how this man meddled with several elections throughout the Americas. Can you think of the last time you came across a situation in the news that was unfamiliar to you? You may not have been aware of the precise cognitive steps you took to access it, but you did have the skills to detect similarities between the new situation and your prior understanding. Each time we successfully transfer our learning to a new situation, there are three essential factors at play.

1. We have an association between a previously learned situation and the novel situation, often linked through organizing ideas or concepts.

2. We have operational schema or patterns of thought about the relationships among these concepts gained from deeper levels of learning within the larger domain.

3. We have the metacognitive skills to monitor our thinking as we detect the similarities and differences from one situation to another.

These factors reveal potential limitations to avoid if we want students to be successful with transferring their learning to a new or novel situation. One limiting factor in fostering transfer lies in pairing the experience with the knowledge base of the learner. If the student has no related knowledge and experiences, transfer is not likely going to happen. As teachers, knowing the learner developmentally and experientially is essential when promoting transfer of learning. It also shows the importance of the deeper learning phase we discussed in Chapter 3—explicitly helping students to build conceptual connections and to become conscious of their thinking and understanding along the way.

Knowing the learner developmentally and experientially is essential when promoting transfer of learning.

Moving From Deep Learning to Transfer

All of the work we do as teachers is for naught if students fail to appropriately transfer their learning. For example, many students struggle to apply their understanding about conflicts, alliances, and sovereignty from one major war to another. One of the concerns is that students (often struggling ones) attempt to transfer *without* detecting similarities and differences, and the transfer does not work (and they see this as evidence that they are dumb). Instead, they memorize facts in isolation to pass tests. Moving on to the next grade level or course is not the true purpose of school, although sadly, many students think it is.

School is a time to apprentice students into the act of becoming their own teachers. We want them to be goal-directed, have the dispositions needed to formulate their own questions, and possess the tools to pursue them. In other words, as their own learning becomes visible to them, we want it to become the catalyst for continued learning, whether the teacher is present or not. However, we don't leave these things to chance. We teach with intention, making sure that students acquire and consolidate the needed concepts, skills, and metacognitive awareness that make self-directed learning possible. By showing students how we ourselves are learners, we in turn model for them how they can teach themselves. Figure 4.1 summarizes the relationship between what we do as teachers and how those teaching behaviors create the conditions for transferring learning.

Transfer is both a goal of learning and a mechanism for propelling learning. Transfer as a goal means that we want students to begin to take the reins of their own learning as they deepen their understanding and be able to unlock situations they encounter beyond the classroom. Transfer is also a mechanism for learning such that students acquire, consolidate, and deepen their knowledge as they move forward and continue to learn. In the next sections, we'll turn our attention to transfer mechanisms. When we have an understanding of how transfer occurs, we can better establish the conditions for ensuring that students meet transfer goals.

Video 4.1
Teaching for Transfer

http://resources.corwin.com/VL-socialstudies

School is a time to apprentice students into the act of becoming their own teachers.

Highly effective teachers . . .	Such that students . . .
Communicate clear learning intentions	Understand the learning intentions
Have challenging success criteria	Are challenged by the success criteria
Teach a range of learning strategies	Develop a range of learning strategies
Know when students are not progressing	Know when they are not progressing
Provide feedback	Seek feedback
Visibly learn themselves	Visibly teach themselves

Source: Hattie, J. (n.d.). *Visible Learning, that make the difference in education* [PowerPoint presentation]. Visible Learning Laboratories, University of Auckland, New Zealand. Retrieved from http://docplayer.net/4137828-Visible-learning-that-make-the-difference-in -education-john-hattie-visible-learning-laboratories-university-of-auckland.html

Figure 4.1

Types of Transfer: Near and Far

As we discussed in Chapter 3, social studies learning can be viewed as a cycle and transfer should be happening often, not just at the end of a lesson or unit. In fact, the goal of *all* learning is transfer as it shows that understanding is involved (Bransford, Brown, & Cocking, 2000). By this, we mean that transfer is more than memorization; it also involves using what we've learned in one setting when we encounter a new setting, and recognition on the part of the learner about what has occurred is essential. It is more helpful to consider this across two dimensions: near transfer and far transfer (Perkins & Salomon, 1992).

Near transfer occurs when the new situation is paired closely with a learned situation. For example, let's take the water crisis on the Nile from the middle school geography course that we looked at in Chapter 1. Students studied the issue from the perspective of Egypt and South Sudan to gain surface level understanding. They consolidated their understanding by looking at the relationships between scarce resources, nations' relative power in the world, and conflict. They could then

Transfer is both a goal of learning and a mechanism for propelling learning.

transfer their understanding to a similar situation where two nations of different levels of power compete over a similar natural resource, such as Turkey and Iraq competing over the Tigris River. The teacher asks students to categorize the elements of the new situation such as the resource, the two nations, and the relative power between the nations. The teacher also models how she dissects the situation and compares the similarities and differences between the two situations.

The size of the leap is larger in *far transfer*, as the learner is able to make connections between more seemingly remote situations. For example, if the geography students transfer their understanding about resource scarcity and conflict to a situation such as the Senkaku (or Diaoyu) Islands in the South China Sea, where China and Japan have been competing for years. The relative level of power between China and Japan is more equal in comparison to the other previous examples, and they are competing over islands off the coasts of their territories, making ownership a bit more convoluted, instead of a single river that flows through each of their countries. The cognitive jump for this transfer is much greater. Ideally, we intentionally structure the learning progression from near to far transfer.

The Paths of Transfer: Low-Road Hugging and High-Road Bridging

So far we have discussed transfer across a continuum from near to far, with the novel situations becoming increasingly remote. However, they remain conceptually similar to one another. Now let's introduce mechanisms, or paths, for transfer: low-road and high-road transfer (Perkins & Salomon, 1992). In this case, the contrastive element is the extent to which the thinking involved is under the learner's conscious direction.

Figure 4.2 summarizes each of these mechanisms.

Let's look back at Mr. Jackson's first-grade class from Chapter 2. Students began acquiring surface level knowledge about roles and responsibilities by considering the common features of these two concepts through

HUGGING AND BRIDGING METHODS FOR LOW-ROAD AND HIGH-ROAD TRANSFER

Hugging to Promote Low-Road Transfer *Students are learning to apply skills and knowledge.*	Bridging to Promote High-Road Transfer *Students are learning to make links across concepts.*
The teacher is associating prior knowledge with new knowledge.	Students are using analogies and metaphors to illustrate connections across disciplines or content.
Students are categorizing information.	Students are deriving rules and principles based on examples.
The teacher is modeling and thinking aloud.	Students are thinking metacognitively and reflectively to plan and organize.
Students are summarizing and rehearsing knowledge.	Students are creating new and original content.
The teacher creates role-play and simulation opportunities for students to apply new knowledge to parallel situations.	Students are applying new knowledge to dissimilar situations.

Figure 4.2

multiple examples—teachers, coaches, principals, students, and parents. They deepened their learning by investigating the relationship between roles and responsibilities in the classroom community. Next, they transferred the relationship between roles and responsibilities to the larger school community—an example of *low-road transfer*.

Their success in transfer was due in part to the increasing automaticity they could draw upon in recognizing roles and responsibilities in different situations. In other words, with growing automaticity came a corresponding decrease in the amount of conscious attention they needed. Mr. Jackson employed a hugging technique by creating these low-road opportunities that stayed close to the original target, allowing students to see the similarities of roles and responsibilities across similar situations. But soon the teacher moved from hugging to a *high-road bridging* technique as he increasingly challenged students to generalize conceptual relationships, including how roles usually have correspond-ing responsibilities to help communities run smoothly.

It is likely that their ability to recognize the interplay between roles and responsibilities in a new situation also required some conscious self-direction about strategies. They may have checked their understanding of roles and responsibilities against the example on the concept wall, or read their previous examples of roles and responsibilities in the class-room context again to see if their observations in a new context made sense, and then compared it to the school community to see if their prior understanding fit in the second new situation. In this case, they are also employing some high-road transfer as they remind themselves to use their previous learning to unlock this new situation. In the pro-cess, their learning is becoming more visible to the students themselves. In those moments, they are taking command of their own learning as they teach themselves.

We intentionally used a Grade 1 example to illustrate transfer because we want to ensure that it is understood that transfer as a mechanism (1) occurs even among the youngest learners and (2) changes in appear-ance as the learner progresses developmentally. Learning transfer is not something that only happens with older learners. So now let's look at evidence of different types of transfer and the use of different paths of transfer, with adolescents in mind.

As we saw in the previous chapter, US history teacher Krista Ferraro has been exploring the relationship between freedom and oppression in her unit on the US Civil War and Reconstruction. But the larger narrative of freedom and oppression is one that they will return to throughout the year. The learning so far is mostly *near transfer* of learning, as Ms. Ferraro has done much of the conceptualization for them. She has selected texts where the relationship between freedom and oppression is very much in evidence. For the most part, she isolated the players they were exploring, namely former slaveholders and newly freed people, Confederate and Union soldiers, state governments and the federal government. As the unit progressed, she frequently reviewed the elements of freedom and oppression so that her students are able to assimilate knowledge and recognize these concepts automatically over time. She also intentionally selected text excerpts that are familiar to her students. Students reread the chapter from the textbook with fresh eyes, a *low-road hugging* technique. Her students increased their skill at recognizing these concepts and the complex interplay between them with increasing automaticity. This in turn freed up cognitive space to attend to the more cognitive demanding task of analyzing a completely new situation.

Ms. Ferraro increases the challenge by asking students to transfer their understanding of the complex interplay between freedom and oppression to the context of US Westward Expansion. She is zooming out beyond the established regions of Northern United States, Southern United States, and the lands of the Louisiana Purchase, and thus enlarging their previous learning beyond slaveholders and enslaved people, Union and Confederate. In addition to these same stakeholders, there are many more concepts, players, and relationships involved in US Westward Expansion—such as new territory, explorers, indigenous populations, recent immigrants, railroad companies, involvement by Mexico and Great Britain, to name a few. The concepts of freedom and oppression in this context are not as easily identifiable. Students begin to make analogies between the two situations of Reconstruction and US Westward Expansion. They begin to derive a more extensive and nuanced understanding of economic and political power and its relationship to nineteenth-century Americans' conception of both freedom and oppression.

They begin to plan their extensive written essays that will be part of their summative assessment. Their learning grows as Ms. Ferraro uses more *high-road bridging* techniques to foster increasingly conceptual thinking. Importantly, her students' learning has become visible to them, as they transform knowledge consciously and with intention. At these times, they have become their own teachers as they make new discoveries themselves.

Like the Nile River example we shared earlier, we can zoom in on two players or concepts at a time in any historical or modern situation when students are acquiring and consolidating initial surface learning of concepts and facts, and then zoom out to widen the scope of the situation we are studying once we get to deep and transfer levels of learning, using the concepts to compare the known situation with the new facts. Social studies teachers likely already think about their courses in a similar way, taking students on the journey of surface learning to acquire and consolidate initial understanding, and then introducing contemporaneous facts and concepts from the same time period to deepen and then transfer learning. We hope this chapter provides additional clarity about how to best help students do this difficult task.

Thus far, we've presented transfer in discrete categories, but in practice, it is not so clear-cut. In other words, there is a continuum between near and far, and between hugging the low road and bridging to the high road. Transfer is what makes it possible for students to acquire and consolidate the surface learning that is foundational for deep learning. As students deepen their learning, we look for them to think in increasingly conceptual ways. When it comes to disciplinary literacy, such as source analysis, we also want them to move from declarative knowledge of the skill (what it is), to procedural knowledge (how to use it), to conditional knowledge (when to use it) (Paris, Lipson, & Wixson, 1983). In the remainder of this chapter, we'll highlight ways to promote transfer toward conceptual learning and disciplinary literacy. Transfer is the conduit, and we can intentionally instruct to cultivate it. This requires establishing the conditions that make it possible and using bridging high-road transfer practices that make it probable.

Setting the Conditions for Transfer of Learning

It should come as no surprise that a major condition for transfer to occur concerns relevancy. Learning becomes more meaningful when learners see what they're learning as being meaningful in their own lives. Relevancy doesn't have to be at the grand level, but it does need to have implications that are developmentally appropriate and are seen as being useful in students' learning lives. Transfer allows students to see how their learning in one situation can be galvanized in new situations.

Video 4.2
Transferring Learning to Real World Situations

http://resources.corwin.com/ VL-socialstudies

As Wineburg (2018) cautions, "Knowledge possessed is not knowledge deployed, especially when such knowledge is deemed irrelevant" (p. 90). When we spend time in the transfer phase, students take ownership of their learning because they see the value.

Those learning intentions and success criteria that we discussed at length in Chapters 1 and 2 are just as important for promoting transfer as they are for fostering initial learning. Although students are engaged in more self-directed tasks during the transfer period, they need goals and ways to measure their progress. Learning intentions in this phase often include more independence such as "We are learning how to recognize similarities and differences between situations we've previously studied and new ones."

Earlier in this book, we talked about how problem-based learning is not effective during surface learning, in large part because students haven't acquired and consolidated the knowledge they need to even begin to analyze and create. But as students deepen their knowledge, introducing them to a problem is a great way to promote transfer by building relevance into what they do. The conditions created by Ms. Ferraro in the US history example allowed for students to think conceptually as they studied fact-rich contexts in history. Younger children can do this as well, as we have seen with several elementary teachers throughout this book.

Teaching Students to Organize Conceptual Knowledge

Transfer allows students to see how their learning in one situation can be galvanized in new situations.

To think more conceptually, students need to figure out how the surface knowledge they have acquired to understand concepts, and the deep knowledge they have developed about how ideas relate to one another, comes more fully under their own command. In large part, students benefit from organizing conceptual knowledge so they can analyze their understanding and identify where they need to go next in their learning. Importantly, a hallmark of transfer of learning is when the student is in the driver's seat.

Identifying Similarities and Differences

In the previous chapters, we wrote about helping students identify the critical attributes of organizing concepts. These concepts work like "coat hangers" in a closet, as new knowledge is draped onto an existing form, and can be easily retrieved later (Hattie, 2012, p. 102). As students move to transfer, teachers are looking for them to locate similarities and differences between and among concepts and situations. This may not happen spontaneously, but can be part of the expectations for how students explain and share information.

Identifying similarities and differences involves comparing two or more things. You will recall graphic organizers and concept maps from Chapter 3. In these examples, typically the teacher gives students two or more items to compare and guides the comparisons. In the transfer phase of learning, we want students to gain more independence in identifying similarities and differences that are temporally or conceptually more removed from one another. At this stage in the learning journey, we want to leave more room for students to select items to compare. For example, Ms. Ferraro could ask her students to compare and contrast any two or more groups from Westward Expansion and Reconstruction. Or she could ask them to compare and contrast the Reconstruction era to any other time period they would like to compare it to. The final important step in this process is asking students to produce a summary of the comparison—usually through a written or oral format—to organize and consolidate learning.

This strategy also involves classifying things into conceptual categories. When we ask students to transfer their learning to a new situation, a useful initial step is to identify the familiar concepts. Students should ask themselves, "What concepts are present in this situation? Where do I see familiar ideas such as power, freedom, conflict, resources, alliances, or opportunities?" This practice can become more familiar and automatic the more we do it, which is the goal for genuine transfer of learning.

Analogies are another way to identify similarities and differences between two or more items. Mr. Jackson asked his first-grade students to make an analogy to how roles and responsibilities work together in a community. The teacher asked, "What other teams work together so that good things happen for everyone involved?" One student with advanced understanding volunteered to make an initial attempt. She connected the topic to a previous unit they studied on plants and pollinators. She said, "Community helpers are kinda like how plants and bees work together to make more plants and honey?" Another student excitedly added, "Yeah, they have different jobs. But they have goals. And they need each other."

Similarly, ancient history teacher Sarah Broden asked her students to make analogies between oligarchy, monarchy, and representative democracy. Students discussed ideas in small groups and then decided on the ones they thought were the best to share with the class. One group relayed their discussion about the analogy of each of these societal structures to middle school students. One student explained, an oligarchy is like when the popular kids try to tell the rest of the class what to do wear, listen to, watch, and stuff. A monarchy is like when the team captain who was picked by the basketball coach leads the team through warm-ups and calls some plays in the games. And a representative democracy is like the student council where the president is voted on by the whole class to represent them.

Ms. Broden was proud of her students. "I couldn't believe it," she said. "Such sophisticated analogies coming from seventh graders made my day and really showed me that they understood these concepts from ancient history."

Video 4.3
Reading Across
Documents
Collaboratively

http://resources.corwin.com/
VL-socialstudies

Reading Across Documents

Another method to facilitate transfer of learning is by having students read, investigate, and write across multiple documents. Many students become adept over time at summarizing the information from a single text, identifying its main arguments, and reporting on key details. But this becomes much more challenging when reading across texts, especially when those texts contain conflicting points of view. The ability to adopt a critical approach to analyzing multiple texts is a mark of a student who is thinking conceptually. On the other hand, those who accept textual information at face value, without questioning its source or seeking corroboration, are at risk for not transferring knowledge. A study of undergraduates who were confronted with multiple documents containing conflicting information about the possible health risks associated with cell phones found that those with a simplistic view of knowledge (i.e., an accumulation of facts) had difficulty processing across texts (Ferguson, Bråten, & Strømsø, 2012).

However, those who understood that doubt and seeking resolution are vital to knowledge building fared much better. In other words, students who held a mental model of how one builds knowledge that included questioning, doubting, investigating, and seeking resolution were able to understand the arguments in the text at a deeper level than those who viewed learning as fact-gathering.

This is an essential skill for history students to master. Advanced Placement tests feature a form of this—document-based questions (DBQ). Students draw from three to over a dozen textual and visual primary source documents to answer a prompt in an on-demand essay. The intention of DBQs is to engage in historical analysis rather than simple retrieval and recall of information. Ideally, the documents chosen differ from one another in tone, perspective, and levels of formality. Analyzing the writing of several authors, each of whom have different writing styles, raises the level of complexity for students.

The need to develop the skill of reading across documents is not confined to high school students. Elementary and middle school students regularly encounter in their textbooks primary source documents positioned next to the main secondary source passages. These documents may include visual information in the form of art, photographs, or maps of the time. Other primary sources include excerpts from personal journals and newspaper articles covering an event. The purpose of utilizing artifacts and evidence from the historical period under study is to provide learners with the experience of corroborating and contextualizing (Wineberg, 1991). The practice of engaging in historical analysis elevates learning from acquisition and consolidation to transformation, essential for transfer of learning. These secondary interpretations encourage students to engage in the critical thinking necessary in history and social studies. However, without the guidance of the teacher, these primary source documents do little more than provide colorful decoration with little thinking beyond, "Oh, that's interesting."

Students in Bella Sales's eighth-grade class examined excerpts from John Quincy Adams's argument to the Supreme Court in 1841 regarding the Amistad case. In 1839, Portuguese slave traders kidnapped people from Sierra Leone and shipped them to a plantation in Cuba on the Amistad in violation of a number of treaties. The captives revolted and took possession of the ship and ordered it to be sailed back to Sierra Leone. However, members of the crew sailed north instead, and when they landed in Connecticut the plantation owners were freed while the captives were imprisoned. The case of the Africans was argued by the former president, who based his argument on the natural rights of all humans to freedom.

Ms. Sales's students read a letter by 11-year-old Kale, a captive on the ship, written to Adams. In it, the boy said, "[A]ll we want is make us free," and argued that he and Adams shared the same desires about love of friends, family, and God. After discussing the boy's letter, the teacher led a close reading of excerpts from Adams's court argument, looking for parallels to points Kale had raised. In particular, they looked for similarities between Kale's assertions and those made by Adams on the human right to fight for one's freedom. The court ruled in favor of the captives seized from Sierra Leone.

The teacher later said, "I want to be sure that my students are regularly confronting evidence that comes from ordinary people of the time, not just major historical figures." Ms. Sales noted, "Sometimes I have them read and discuss counterpoints to the prevailing wisdom of the time. In this case, I wanted them to see that Adams is amplifying the perspectives of the people he was representing."

Jigsaw

Jigsaw is one of the powerful strategies that we can use across sur-face, deep, and transfer levels of learning. As we saw in Chapter 2, second-grade teacher Michelle DiMarzio asked students to complete a jigsaw activity about the culture of four different African nations. At that stage of learning, she wanted students to both acquire their understanding of the culture of these nations and also to consolidate their understanding of the concept of *culture*. Students first met in their *expert groups* and studied the same country all together. Next, they went to their second groups, the mixed groups, to teach each other about the different countries they studied. In the deeper learning phase, students completed graphic organizers comparing the cultures of the four different countries. At the transfer phase of this activity, she asked them to return to their original expert groups and discuss what they noticed about how their original country's culture compared to the others and what this meant for the cul-ture of the broader continent of Africa. In this phase, students were thinking about their thinking and synthesizing their previous ideas about culture.

Most student groups reached the conclusion that the similarities seemed greater than the differences among the four countries they studied. Ms. DiMarzio asked students to discuss how the culture of different countries can be so similar on the same continent. Because she had previously taught students how to make analogies, students brought in this strategy automatically. One student compared the con-tinent of Africa with different countries to the way the United States is one country made up of many different states. He continued to explain, "In the United States, we like a lot of the same sports, kind of like how soccer is a favorite sport among many different countries in Africa." Another student compared a continent and different countries to money. "You can make a dollar with different cents. You have coins that are different, but they are all cents and they can all add up to one dollar." Once students have command of the topics we are teaching them, even young students can make these sophisticated connections and observations.

EFFECT SIZE FOR
JIGSAW = 1.20

Teaching Students to Transform Conceptual Knowledge

As students transfer their learning at the conceptual level, they learn *when* to use the knowledge they have or are pursuing. This conditional or strategic use of knowledge quickens the pace of the learning, and as such, the line between organizing and transforming conceptual knowledge is blurred. For example, Ms. DiMarzio's second-grade students moved rapidly back and forth as they organized and transformed knowledge about the cultures of different countries in Africa. This is true learning at its best, as students oscillate among surface, deep, and transfer learning, made all the easier as they deepen their understanding of a concept. Keep in mind that knowledge begets knowledge, and one of the strongest predictors of a learner's future capacity to learn is what he or she already knows (Murphy & Alexander, 2002). Jigsaw activities, such as the one described in the previous section, suggest how seamlessly students can move from organizing to transforming knowledge. Additional learning opportunities listed in this section can furnish students with the forums they need, as they become their own self-directed teachers.

Debates

In Chapter 1, we noted that our challenge as educators is not to just identify what works, as almost everything works for some students at some time, especially when zero growth is expected. Rather, we need to match what works to *accelerate* student learning, and then implement it at the right time (Hattie, 2009). Formal class discussions such as debates are one such practice. This strategy has the added benefit of helping students to practice important civic skills that they will hopefully use in their lives.

Class discussions, as discussed in Chapter 3, deepen student learning. Those are often a bit informal, even if we ask students to prepare in advance. The goals in informal class discussions that deepen learning are to listen, take in ideas, and consider multiple points of view. The goal for debates is to persuade and refute counterarguments made about controversial issues. Both are important for high-quality social studies learning that promotes democratic civic life.

We have witnessed scores of students transform from shy, self-conscious young people into powerful, confident thinkers with expansive content knowledge and conceptual understanding in social studies through programs such as the National Association for Urban Debate Leagues program or the Middle School Public Debate Program, designed by Shuster and Meany (2005). Formal classroom debates can dramatically enhance any social studies learning environment. This fast-paced, oral, public showcase of thinking will improve student writing when it comes time for written essays.

Debates should occur once students have acquired and consolidated both surface learning and deep learning of the social studies content that will underpin the debate topic. At this point, they are ready to debate one or more controversial statements, often called *motions*, related to the broad topic and organizing concepts of study. They should be given time to prepare, where they will often review notes and find more details beyond what they've previously studied in class. We also find it helpful, especially for younger students, to practice the debate structure with a less controversial topic such as "Year-round education should be required for all students" so that they get the feel of the format before introducing a more polarizing social studies topic. Formal classroom discussions such as debates expand students' deliberation skills, understanding of various points of view, civic knowledge, and interest in civic life (Hess & McAvoy, 2014).

After conducting debates a few times over the school year, Ms. Ferraro asked her US history students to prepare for a debate on reparations and an official apology to African Americans for slavery. Students analyzed an article illustrating strong opposition from a majority of Americans surveyed on public opinion polls about reparations and apologies for slavery (Swanson, 2014) and read an article making a case for reparations (Coates, 2014). She also provided a class period and homework time to conduct further research on their arguments. Because this is such a controversial issue, Ms. Ferraro asked them to prepare both sides of the debate. They were randomly selected to present one side the first day and then the other side the next day.

As Burek and Losos (2014) note, "Similar to a trial, the debate opens and closes with the burden of proof on the proposition" (p. 50). The format of the debate usually begins and ends with the proposition side, with each student responsible for a single two- minute speech:

- First Proposition speaker
- First Opposition speaker
- Second Proposition speaker
- Second Opposition speaker
- Opposition Rebuttal speaker
- Proposition Rebuttal speaker

We find it helpful to ask students to take notes as their team presents, so that they can follow the lines of arguments and attempt to specifically refute the arguments of the opposing side. The Urban Debate League calls these *flow sheets* and even first and second speakers can pass notes to the rebuttal speaker to further participate after their turn has passed.

Extended Writing

Writing is the result of knowledge construction. Evidence of a student's transfer of knowledge can be found in the extended writing pieces he or she creates. Writing instruction, like reading, is a constellation of approaches, as students move from ideas (surface), to thinking (deep), to constructing knowledge (transfer). While the effect size overall for writing programs is a decent 0.43, understand that this covers quite a bit of territory. Embedded within effective writing instruction is teaching students to summarize as part of their study skills and engage in careful planning by mapping concepts. As such, young students learn about writing processes initially as a series of discrete steps, but should move quickly into the thinking that is required of writers as they plan, organize, and revise their original writing.

Writing instruction is also a constellation of effective teaching practices. The feedback loop between the teacher and peers is critical as students immersed in writing seek and offer feedback from others. And don't overlook the importance of a writer's understanding of the goal. Like other elements of learning, writers benefit from clear learning intentions and success criteria related to the audience, the purpose, and the format (Graham & Perin, 2007). In other words, the way that writing is taught and guided makes a significant difference in how well students are able to use this as an expression of their construction of knowledge.

Whether students are writing a poetic analysis in English class or answering a document-based question prompt in world history, the ability to interpret, synthesize, and communicate knowledge remains the same. Writing is one of the primary ways that students are asked to make meaning and is a skillset that's transferable across disciplines. Considering it's a recursive process, there's ample opportunity for students to not only refine their writing, but their thinking as well.

Middle school teacher Jeff Philips asks his students to transfer what they have learned about government and economic systems by creating their own society and explaining how that society would respond to various global issues. "The issues themselves are modeled after real world events, so the students feel a sense of legitimacy as they try and tackle the issues with their created country," Jeff explained.

Students first write about how their country was shaped by the relationships with other countries, trade, and their stances on social issues. They use this analysis to help them respond to a given scenario that takes a real-world event—such as migrants coming to the border—and asks them to respond as the leader of their nation. Students add to their country profile by writing their response and the reasons for making it. The response has to include connections to their beliefs as a leader and the historical influences their nation has faced through the previous weeks of society building. The reasons they use to justify their responses come from the relationships with other countries, the wants and needs of their citizens, and the nation's historical stance on various social issues. Jeff described what happened when asking students to transfer their learning through extended writing: "Students applied their prior understanding of how countries around the world responded to these large-scale social issues when writing their responses. This assessment forced them to take their surface and deep levels of understanding and transfer it to a new situation, one that has tangible analogues in the real world."

When high school history teachers Brittany Giovenelli and Debbie Siler plan cross-content units with English teacher Trevor Aleo, their first step is to ensure they're exploring similar skills and concepts in their instruction. By establishing a common cross-content vocabulary, they ensure that students will be able to leverage the writing skills learned in each class.

"The first step is to get students thinking and talking about the concepts we're exploring in both of our classes." Trevor Aleo said. "By intentionally connecting the information we're teaching in both our courses, and explicitly articulating the relationship between our focal concepts, we equip students with a wider knowledge base for students to work from."

For example, while reading *Lord of the Flies* in English and learning about the French Revolution in world history, both classes organize the events of their texts around the concepts of chaos, power, order, and control. Students actively make connections between the events in the novel and history, and are encouraged to transfer their understanding back and forth across content areas.

In addition to exploring similar ideas, both English and history classes take a similar approach to the writing process—affording students ample time and practice to find voice and volume through frequent low-stakes writing. Though different content areas have students write for different purposes, the ability to communicate through exceptional word choice and flowing, organized prose is the same. The more students write, the more comfortable they are articulating themselves. Engaging in this process across content lines makes it twice as powerful.

Both sets of teachers also use similar planning and brainstorming activities to get students mapping their writing before they begin. Students use sticky notes and whiteboards to visualize the structure, sequence, and connections within their writing. This allows them to think through their writing before they respond to more complex prompts or assignments. By using the same methodology in both social studies and English, students develop and harness a flexible skillset instead of learning multiple, isolated strategies that never quite stick.

By empowering students to think critically and across content, encouraging them to write for voice and volume, and helping them develop a flexible brainstorming protocol, students are set up with success.

Conclusion

"I am a change agent."

This Visible Learning mind frame isn't a platitude. In the hands of an effective teacher, visible teaching and learning center our practices. It's true that some students will engage in transfer learning without any of us paying much attention to it, but that signals a lost opportunity as well. The keyword in the first sentence is *agent*. As teachers, we have the potential for tremendous agency—to make learning happen—if we'd only seize the chance to do so. Being a change agent means bearing witness to student learning, reflecting on it, and recognizing that student progress tells us something about ourselves. How will we ever know what students are truly capable of if we don't get deeply involved in their learning lives?

This last question has implications for assessment, which is the subject of the next chapter. As we have written before, a staggering majority of what is assessed requires surface-level knowledge, thus reinforcing to students that we only care about factual and declarative knowledge. But it's really difficult to assess for deep and transfer learning if we rarely witness it occurring. How can we assess students when we don't really know the limits of what they can achieve?

DETERMINING IMPACT, RESPONDING, AND KNOWING WHAT DOES NOT WORK

5

What criteria do you use to evaluate a lesson? Do you pay attention to students' body language to gauge whether or not they are interested? Picture a class where students are making trifold display boards about a specific aspect of World War II. There are photos, flags, maps, glue sticks, markers, and lots of other art supplies strewn about. Students seem to be on-task and enjoying the activity of creating their own displays.

In this example, we're pleased to see that students seem to be enjoying the activity and are paying attention to the task at hand. It's important that students experience joy at school. And attention is a necessary condition for learning. But we expect more. Lessons should impact students' learning. It's insufficient to simply say that a lesson was good (or bad) and that students were engaged (or were not). We often chase the holy grail of engagement without paying sufficient attention to learning. In fact, we believe that it is teachers' professional responsibility to determine the extent to which the lessons they develop and deliver impact students' learning. Thus far in this book, we have focused on what works best to accelerate learning from a research perspective. Putting each of the approaches we've discussed into practice is likely to ensure better learning, especially when specific strategies are linked with the specific phase of learning students need.

> When the desired impact is not achieved, effective teachers take action.

But we don't leave this to chance or make the assumption that there will be an impact. We test it. We evaluate it. And when the desired impact is not achieved, effective teachers take action.

Determining Impact

Video 5.1
Measuring Impact

http://resources.corwin.com/ VL-socialstudies

Way back in Chapter 1, we discussed effect sizes. As you probably recall, an effect size is a quantitative measure of the strength of a phenomenon. In other words, it tells us how powerful something is in creating change. And, as you probably recall, an effect size of 0.40 (calculated with Cohen's d) suggests that the student(s) gained about a year's worth of growth for a year in school. The implication is that 0.40 should be the expectation for instruction and intervention. In other words, students should gain at least a year's worth of learning for each year they are in school. An effect size of less than 0.40 suggests that the instruction or intervention was less than effective and may warrant change or revision. At the very minimum, an effect size below 0.40 begs for a discussion about the effort.

The effect size tool can be applied at the classroom level as well. Teachers can calculate effect sizes for their classes and individual students to determine the impact their instruction and intervention have had. This builds teachers' sense of efficacy, which is the belief in their ability to positively impact student learning. Jerald (2007) noted that teachers with strong self-efficacy

- tend to exhibit greater levels of planning and organization,

- are more open to new ideas and are more willing to experiment with new methods to better meet the needs of their students,

- are more persistent and resilient when things do not go smoothly,

- are less critical of students when they make errors, and

- are less inclined to refer a difficult student to special education. (Protheroe, 2008, p. 43)

Over time, as teachers discuss the data and success with their peers, they develop collective teacher efficacy. Goddard, Hoy, and Hoy (2000) define collective teacher efficacy as "the perceptions of teachers in a school that the efforts of the faculty as a whole will have a positive effect on students" (p. 480), with teachers agreeing that "teachers in this school can get through to the most difficult students" (p. 480).

Importantly, perceptions are formed based on our experiences. When teachers experience success collaborating with peers and those collaborations improve teaching and learning, they notice. It is the evidence of impact that feeds collective efficacy. These accumulated data points become the collective efficacy researchers note is powerful (Hoy, Sweetland, & Smith, 2002). We're just saying that the definition of success, on which these perceptions and thus collective teacher efficacy are built, should include student learning.

Student learning at the classroom level can be held to the same standard as researchers, an effect size of at least 0.40. Having said that, we recognize that many classroom assessments do not have the psychometric properties of assessments used in most research studies and thus the claim that 0.40 is equivalent to about a year may be questioned. But, it's a starting point to help teachers determine if they are having an impact.

> Students should gain at least a year's worth of learning for each year they are in school.

The process of calculating an effect size is fairly simple. Before we discuss that, it's important to remember a few things:

1. *Lessons should have clear learning intentions.* It's hard to determine whether students have learned something if they (and we) aren't sure what it was they were supposed to learn.

2. *Lessons should have clear success criteria.* The success criteria provide the tools necessary to assess learning. If the success criteria involve writing about history, then learning has to involve both writing and content-area learning. Sometimes teachers conflate success criteria and are unable to determine if students have learned something, even when they have.

3. *The success criteria indicate what quality looks like.* To determine whether or not learning has occurred, students and teachers have to know what success looks like. As Collins (2001)

noted, good is the enemy of great. If students believe that good enough is sufficient, they may only reach for that level. When they understand what excellent work looks like, they can reach higher.

4. *Students should know where they stand in relation to the criteria for success.* When students have no idea if they've done well or not, learning is compromised. Students should understand that learning is on a continuum, that errors are opportunities to learn, and that they can learn more.

With these four conditions in place, teachers are ready to examine the impact of the learning experience.

Pre-Assessment

It starts with a pre-assessment, or progress testing as it is sometimes called.

Without a pre-assessment, we cannot determine if learning occurred. When teachers only use post-assessments, such as end-of-unit tests, essays, or projects, they will know who has demonstrated the expected level of achievement (and who has not), but they won't know who has learned because learning is a measure of change over time.

> Without a pre-assessment, we cannot determine if learning occurred.

It's easy to overlook the pre-assessment and accept achievement as learning. But without it, becoming a better teacher and designer of amazing learning situations is left to chance. For example, Todd Hanson assessed his students during the last week of October on their abilities to identify major locations on a map. He found that most but not all students were able to accurately place all of the locations on the assessment. This was their current achievement, but it didn't tell him anything about his own impact because he did not have a baseline. What if the majority of the students could already do this in September? In that case, the time he spent teaching these locations was a waste. But what if none of them could locate these places in September? In that case, the lessons were likely pretty powerful, and he may want to share them with his team. This example highlights a missing part of many teachers' instructional practices. Failing to identify what students know and can do at the outset of a unit of study blocks any ability to determine if learning has occurred and thus any ability for there to be a discussion about effective instruction and intervention.

Armed with baseline, pre-assessment information, teachers can design instructional interventions to close the gap between what students already know and what they are expected to learn. In this case, time is used more precisely because specific strategies can be selected based on the type of learning needed. Students who have a need for surface-level learning are probably not going to do well with a series of problem-based learning lessons. On the other hand, students who need deep consolidation learning are probably not going to benefit from learning mnemonics.

Post-Assessment

Once the lessons have been completed, teachers readminister the outcome measure. This opens the door to an investigation about impact. Did the lessons that were taught change students? That is learning.

When the pre- and posttest data are available, the effect size can be determined.

As an example, Figure 5.1 contains the source analysis writing rubric scores from a middle school social studies class. Social studies specialist, Vince Bustamante, along with teacher Rebecca West use a 10-point rubric so they can provide more precise information for students about their development. The rubric includes descriptors for the interpretation and analysis of source-based material, as well as descriptors for grammar and mechanics control.

In the source analysis example, the average pre-assessment score was 5.69. After four weeks of work on understanding traits and attributes of political cartoons, receiving feedback (not error correction), and practicing the skill of analysis of sources the students in Ms. West's class increased to an average 6.71 on the 10-point rubric. Is that a worthy impact? It's hard to judge because a 1.02-point average growth doesn't sound very impressive, so you need to calculate the effect size.

EXAMPLE EFFECT SIZES FOR MIDDLE SCHOOL STUDENTS

Name	Pre-Assessment	Post-Assessment	Individual Effects Sizes
Georgio A	4	5	0.47
Arien A	9.5	10	0.23
Bertin A	7	7	0.00
Ryan C	3	3	0.00
Daniella E	4	5	0.47
Eirin F	2	4	0.93
Charles G	6	6	0.00
Emma L	4	5	0.47
Mariah L	9	10	0.47
Emma M	9	9	0.00
Ameer N	6	7	0.47
Isaiah O	3	5	0.93
Beluchi O	6	7	0.47
Dolly O	5	6	0.47
Mariana R	6	6	0.00
Ethan S	7	6	-0.47
Charis U	3	7	1.87
Akwa U	4	8	1.87
Christian V	4	7	1.40
Sophia Z	9	9	0.00
Dana K	9	9	0.00
Average	5.69	6.71	
Standard Deviation	2.37	1.93	2.15
Effect Size	0.47		

Figure 5.1

To calculate an effect size, first determine the average for the posttest and the average for the pretest. It's easy to do this in an Excel spreadsheet. Here's how:

- Type the students' names in one column.

- Type their scores for the pre- and post-assessments in other columns.

- Highlight the column with the pre-assessment scores and select the *average* tool and place the average at the bottom of that column.

- Do the same for the post-assessment column.

The next step in determining the effect size is to calculate standard deviation. Excel will do this as well*:

1. Type =STDEV.P and then select the student scores in the pre-assessment column again.

2. Do the same in the post-assessment column.

3. Subtract the pre-assessment from the post-assessment and then divide by the standard deviation.

Here's the formula:

$$\text{Effect size} = \frac{\text{Average (post - assessment)} - \text{Average (pre - assessment)}}{\text{Average standard deviation or SD} *}$$

In the source analysis example found in Figure 5.1, the standard deviation for the pre-assessment is 2.37 and the standard deviation for the post-assessment is 1.93. The average of the two is 2.15. When the effect size is calculated using the formula above, it comes to 0.07, above our threshold of 0.40. Thus, Ms. West can conclude her efforts to improve her students' source analysis skills were impactful. She can then infer that the focus on understanding traits and attributes of political cartoons,

*For links to websites for calculating effect sizes, visit our companion website: http://resources .corwin.com/VL-socialstudies.

receiving feedback, and practice worked. As a note of caution, effect sizes do not establish causation. Ms. West cannot say with confidence that these specific actions caused the writing to be better, but she should be encouraged to share her approach with others so that they can determine the impact it might have on their students.

You may have noticed that the effect size is the average for the group. Ms. West really should say that the efforts to improve source analysis worked on average. That's why we suggest that teachers calculate effect sizes for individual students. It's pretty simple to do: subtract an individual student's pre-assessment score from his or her post-assessment score and divide by the average standard deviation.

The formula looks like this:

$$\text{Effect size} = \frac{\substack{\text{Individual score (post-assessment)} - \\ \text{Individual score (pre-assessment)}}}{\text{Average standard deviation or SD for the class}}$$

In this case, many of the students are above the threshold of 0.40. Charis, Akwa, Eirin, and Isaiah really responded to the instruction they received. For these students, Ms. West should reflect on what was optimal about their learning.

As she noted, "These students began participating more in class discussions as the content transitioned from basic level understanding to more current events and issues that directly impact them. Not only were they working on areas of interest but they had a responsibility to others to gain more knowledge." Unfortunately, there was no effect on Charles. As Ms. West noted, "Charles is an English Language Learner so for him to be able to improve on writing assignments, overall, he needs to increase his language acquisition skills, which is a larger battle when coming into high level of understanding, such as analyzing political cartoons."

Ethan experienced regression. His scores declined, and the effect sizes were very low. Ms. West, reflecting on her instruction, said, "Class structure has become more relaxed as they have been working through more hands-on assignments, notably our debate project. As a result, I believe they have did not use class time effectively when given time to practice this skill acquisition. This didn't work, and I owe it to them to schedule some additional instruction so that I can figure out what they need from me." Calculating an effect size allows us accurate data to inform these important conversations. Without it, we are less precise about which students are learning as a result of our instruction, and which are not.

Regularly Checking for Understanding

Conducting pre- and posttests and calculating effect size are vital for more exact measurement of how much growth our students have made as a result of our teaching practices. But this process should accompany frequent and routine checks for understanding, preferably daily. Teachers— and students themselves—should be detectives of student thinking and understanding. Nearly all of the examples provided in the previous chapters can be used as formative assessment data, provided that teachers believe they are continuous evaluators of their own impact and are intentional about using assessment data to inform next steps on instruction.

For instance, to help them consolidate surface learning, students can periodically participate in timed review of material such as map skills or vocabulary quizzes. Perhaps they can self-assess upon completion and record their scores in their notebooks. This activity can be repeated every few lessons so that students try to "best themselves" by improving their scores. Results often follow when students play learning games such as Pictionary or charades with key terms, events, or concepts (Marzano & Pickering, 2005). Teachers can use this formative data to determine the next course of action in lesson planning.

Video 5.2
Checking for
Understanding

http://resources.corwin.com/
VL-socialstudies

How often do your students in your class write, preferably with pen to paper?

Once students have acquired surface level learning, they should be writing short responses to questions and prompts in order to demonstrate their understanding of topics and concepts—and teachers should circulate, reading over students' shoulders, targeting different students each time. Visible learning requires that we make student learning observable. We need students to put their thinking out into the world so that we can determine the impact of our teaching. Asking students to respond with short written paragraphs generally does not happen with enough frequency in social studies classrooms.

Responding When There Is Insufficient Impact

Sometimes, despite our best efforts, students fail to respond to quality instruction. The only way to know if this has occurred is to regularly assess the impact we are having on students. When the impact is less than desirable, effective teachers try something different. They do not simply reteach the same lesson, perhaps slower or louder, hoping that students will get something out of it the second time around. Instead, they examine what worked and what didn't work, talk with colleagues, and redesign the learning opportunities for students.

For example, middle-school teacher Niyesha Turner was in the midst of a unit on separation of powers when she realized that many students were failing to grasp the concept. The students could name all three branches of government and identify different levels such as local, state, and federal governments. But when she asked them to write about the reasons why we might separate powers and analyze the pros and cons, more than half of her students could not adequately explain their answers.

Ms. Turner met with her instructional coach, Nichelle Pinkney to discuss ideas for reteaching this important concept. They settled on the strategy of presenting different situations where a separation in power resulted in increased protection of rights—such as when the police need to present evidence to a judge or jury in order to obtain a warrant before searching someone's house. She presented four different scenarios and asked students to first recognize the different powers, which they could do easily, and then discuss in small groups how the separation of powers was related to individual rights.

They did one together as a whole class before she released them to work in groups.

On the next assessment, students made significant gains on their ability to explain the relevance of this concept, and provide examples from class to prove their explanations. Ms. Turner remarked, "I usually revert to reexplaining the concept and try to explain it in a different way. The formative assessment helped me realize that they could define separation of powers, but couldn't explain its significance. I knew that I needed to show them examples of its relevance in different scenarios so that they could determine the overall pattern of why power is separated in democracies."

Teachers can engage in this type of response on a regular basis. Teaching is about making adjustments and trying to determine what will work for a particular group of students. As we have noted, there is no one right way to teach, and there are a lot of things that teachers do that are effective. Designing learning opportunities, monitoring for impact, and then making adjustments are the hallmark of effective teachers. But there are more formal ways to monitor impact.

Response to Intervention

The evidence for response to intervention (RTI) is significant; it's one of the top influences studied thus far with an effect size of 1.09. In other words, it works. There are several components of an effective RTI effort, which combine to produce the impact seen in the studies. These include universal screening, quality core instruction, progress monitoring, and supplemental and intensive interventions. Entire books have been written on RTI (e.g., Fisher & Frey, 2010), so this section will only highlight the key components necessary for teachers to understand.

EFFECT SIZE FOR RESPONSE TO INTERVENTION = 1.09

Screening

For RTI efforts to be most effective, school staff members have to screen students at the outset of the year. These screening tools are typically quick checks to identify students who may need additional intervention. In the realm of social studies, there are fewer screening tools available than there are for mathematics and literacy. However, a solid grasp of social studies requires strong literacy skills, so perhaps your school may use one of these to examine students' literacy abilities at the start of the year. A more comprehensive list of screening tools can be found at www.rti4success.org/resources/tools-charts/screening-tools -chart. Figure 5.2 contains an essential task list for progress monitoring to help guide you in your efforts.

ESSENTIAL TASK LIST FOR SCREENING TOOLS

Directions: In the second column, write the name(s) of the individual or team who will assume responsibility for the task identified in the first column. In the third column, write the deadline or status of the task.

Task	Responsible Individual/Team	Timeline/Status
Review your screening instrument's items to be certain that content is aligned with the curriculum for each grade level.		
Once a tool has been selected, determine and secure the resources required to implement it.		
Determine initial professional development needs and continuing professional development support.		
Administer the screening measure three times a year (e.g., early fall, midterm, and late spring).		
Create a database that aligns with the screening instrument to hold student information and scores.		
Organize the screening results (e.g., graphs and tables) to provide a profile of all students and their comparisons with each other.		
Monitor results at the classroom level and make decisions about when teachers/instructional programs require more scrutiny and support.		
Add screening results to a database so that students' performance can be monitored over time.		
Specify written steps to follow when further scrutiny is needed for students judged to be at risk.		

Source: Johnson, E., Mellard, D.F., Fuchs, D., & McKnight, M.A. (2006). *Responsiveness to intervention (RTI): How to do it.* Lawrence, KS: National Research Center on Learning Disabilities. Public Domain.

[Download template at resources.corwin.com/VL-socialstudies]

Figure 5.2

For example, the staff at St. John's Elementary use a graded vocabulary inventory and a writing sample to identify students who may potentially need additional instruction and intervention. The teachers focus on direct instruction for the students who are at risk of not meeting expectations. Direct instruction requires that the teacher set clear learning targets and then provide students with explicit instruction followed by practice on each target. The focus at St. John's is on developing students' vocabulary and writing skills because the teachers realize that some of their students, especially those who may have lacked back and forth conversations in early childhood, may benefit from systematic vocabulary and writing work.

Quality Core Instruction

RTI efforts are based on the expectation that students receive quality core instruction as part of their ongoing participation in school. Also known as good first teaching, quality core instruction comprises Tier 1 of the RTI efforts. It's unreasonable to expect that all students receive supplemental and intensive interventions—there isn't time or money for that. If the vast majority of students are not being impacted by the regular classroom environment, we suggest that the tenets in this book may not be in place. In school systems that implement high-quality instruction, based on the influences on achievement outlined in this book, and then monitor the impact of those actions, fewer and fewer students need the extensive support offered through RTI. To our thinking, quality core instruction includes at least the following:

- Teacher clarity on, and communication about, the learning intentions and success criteria

- Student ownership of the expectations for learning

- Positive, humane, growth-producing teacher–student relationships

- Modeling and direct instruction of content

- Collaborative learning opportunities on a daily basis

- Small group learning based on instructional needs rather than perceived ability

- Spaced (rather than mass) independent practice and application of content

These are easy to write, and obvious to many, but not yet common in classrooms around the world. When these actions become the norm in classrooms, the need for additional interventions declines, and students learn more and better.

Progress Monitoring

As previously described, we can calculate effect size to determine impact on learning. Teachers can ascertain whether or not the lessons they designed and delivered made a difference. And then, of course, they can take action. In RTI, teachers also monitor the progress, but they do so with two types of tools:

- Curriculum-based measurements (CBMs) are standardized assessments that have specific directions. These are usually timed and have specific scoring guidelines. CBMs are criterion-based tools that measure mastery of a skill. In essence, the tools help teachers determine if students have met the threshold, or criteria, established by the test maker. Nearly all locations (e.g. states in the United States, provinces in Canada, etc.) have milestone assessments for certain grade levels in social studies. For example, the teachers in Forsyth County Schools use retired end-of-course assessment questions as formative assessment data of their students' progress. They know that many of these questions typically remain at the surface level of learning, so they don't view the assessment as the end goal of their teaching. But they also know that these social studies assessments often measure foundational knowledge, so they look for patterns or trends in students' responses. Importantly, they do not drill dates or names of people when students are missing key knowledge, but rather they refer back to the strategies in Chapter 2 to ensure they are using high-yield strategies with an increased likelihood of success. When they figure out what might be impeding consolidation of knowledge, they can address it and continue to monitor progress.

- Curriculum-based assessments (CBAs) are tools developed by teachers that align with the content they have taught. As Deno (1987) noted, CBAs involve "direct observation and recording of a student's performance in the local curriculum as a basis for gathering information to make instructional decisions" (p. 41). The teachers at Rosa Parks Elementary School use their weekly source analysis quiz as one of their CBAs. They collect and analyze data weekly, taking note of which students struggle with the different moves involved in analyzing a source, and intervene before it's too late. The Rosa Parks teachers favor self-corrected quizzes as an intervention, where students review their work as the teacher conducts a think-aloud using the document camera in the front of the room. They have found that nearly every student develops the skills of source analysis over the course of the year. The interventions are immediate and based on the specific disciplinary literacy skill that a given student did not learn.

Notice that in each case, the progress-monitoring tools that teachers use can result in students receiving supplemental or intensive interventions. Screening tools are important to identify students in need at the outset of the year, but progress-monitoring tools ensure that students are noticed throughout the year. Figure 5.3 contains a series of reflection questions that school teams can ask themselves about their progress monitoring efforts.

Supplemental and Intensive Interventions

In each of the examples we have provided thus far in this chapter, the teachers organized additional interventions for students who demonstrated a need. Students were not left to figure it out on their own, nor did their teachers simply move on, accepting that some students failed to learn. RTI focuses efforts on providing evidence-based interventions for students who do not respond to quality core instruction (also known as Tier 1). In the language of RTI, students can receive Tier 2 or Tier 3 interventions, or a combination of both. This multitier system of support can result in improved student learning. It requires that teachers notice when students do not respond (when the impact is insufficient) and then change the instruction or intervention to reach the desired outcome. The two levels of response are as follows:

1. Tier 2, also known as supplemental interventions

2. Tier 3, also known as intensive interventions

In each of Danny Basma's middle-school classes, a few students have been identified on an initial screening tool as needing additional instruction or intervention in reading comprehension. Mr. Basma does not simply send these students to the school's reading intervention specialist and shrug it off as "not his problem," as he knows that building students' background

ESSENTIAL TASK LIST FOR PROGRESS MONITORING IN TIER 1

Directions: In the second column, write the name(s) of the individual or team who will assume responsibility for the task identified in the first column. In the third column, write the deadline or status of the task.

Task	Responsible Individual/Team	Timeline/Status
Within the relevant content area, review the progress monitoring measure or tool selected for Tier 1 to determine whether content is aligned with your curriculum.		
Once a tool has been selected, determine and secure the resources required to implement it (e.g., computers, folders/copies, testing areas).		
Determine initial professional development needs and continuing professional development support.		
Implement a system of data collection and progress monitoring that includes determining both level and growth rate.		
Administer the progress monitoring measure frequently enough to assess a learner's responsiveness. At Tier 1, screening is three times a year, with routine monitoring weekly or twice weekly.		
Monitor results at the individual student level and make decisions about reasonable cut scores to determine movement to Tier 2 and beyond.		
Monitor results at the classroom level and make decisions about when teachers or instructional programs require more scrutiny and support.		

Source: Johnson, E., Mellard, D.F., Fuchs, D., & McKnight, M.A. (2006). *Responsiveness to intervention (RTI): How to do it.* Lawrence, KS: National Research Center on Learning Disabilities.

[Download template at resources.corwin.com/VL-socialstudies]

Figure 5.3

knowledge about social studies is a key part of increasing their reading comprehension. Instead, Mr. Basma teams up with the reading specialist to make a game plan to maximize their efforts. Together, they outline a list of comprehension strategies and corresponding content knowledge that will increase the students' abilities to comprehend social studies texts. Mr. Basma meets with these students on a weekly basis to provide small group, needs-based instruction. The rest of the class works collaboratively. When these students are not with Mr. Basma, they are working collaboratively with their peers, and other students are meeting with their teacher who focuses on other skills based on the formative assessments.

Ayo Magwood, high school government and history teacher, created a powerful strategy for reaching students who had a difficult time with some of the abstract concepts—liberty, rule of law, limited government—contained in her course work. She helped students who were struggling to grasp these ideas by getting to know their activities and interests outside of school. She then started her small-group work with these students by using a very concrete example of the lesson's concept in their personal lives. For example, the school was debating its uniform policy and students had strong opinions about this. Ms. Magwood linked that to the concepts of liberty and order, and how many public policies can seem like a tension between these two concepts. Then, she highlighted the attributes that this example had and linked it to the unit's content. Next, she asked students to think about additional examples from their lives that shared those attributes.

She shared, "This process resulted in significantly deeper levels of understanding and engagement and transformed my students' ability to keep up with their peers."

The impact that Mr. Basma and Ms. Magwood had on countless students was significant. Their ability to rally resources around students in need, while not neglecting the education of others, is a model for visible learning in social studies. They didn't accept low levels of learning; they implemented actions they believed would result in learning, and they monitored and adjusted to obtain the impact they expected.

Of course, RTI can be implemented on a much wider scale than one teacher's class. Figure 5.4 includes a list of tasks that should be noted as

ESSENTIAL TASK LIST FOR PROGRESS MONITORING IN TIERS 2 AND 3

Directions: In the second column, write the name(s) of the individual or team who will assume responsibility for the task identified in the first column. In the third column, write the deadline or status of the task.

Task	Responsible Individual/Team	Timeline/Status
Implement a system of data collection and progress monitoring that includes determining both level and growth rate.		
Within the relevant area of focus for the intervention, review the progress monitoring measure or tool selected for Tier 2 and beyond to determine whether content is aligned with the intervention.		
Administer the progress monitoring measure frequently enough to assess a learner's responsiveness. At Tier 2, two to five times per week is the research-based recommendation.		
Organize results to provide a profile of the student's progress within this tier. This could be a graph of test scores supplemented with student work samples.		
Monitor results to determine whether a student is responding to the intervention.		
Develop decision rules about when to return a student to Tier 1, when to continue with Tier 2 and beyond, and whether further scrutiny of student performance for special education is warranted.		

Source: Johnson, E., Mellard, D.F., Fuchs, D., & McKnight, M.A. (2006). *Responsiveness to intervention (RTI): How to do it.* Lawrence, KS: National Research Center on Learning Disabilities.

[Download template at resources.corwin.com/VL-socialstudies]

Figure 5.4

teachers and school teams monitor students' progress in Tiers 2 and 3. In some schools, this is done collaboratively, at the grade or department level. Note the collective teacher efficacy involved as groups of teachers examine the impact they have had and then design interventions to ensure that all students learn.

Supplemental and intensive interventions have the potential to positively impact students' learning when they are based on accurate assessment data and when students have instruction that addresses their needs. In general, Tier 2 interventions involve the teacher meeting with small groups of students while the rest of the class completes other tasks. Importantly, we hope that the implementation of RTI does not mean that the rest of the class is assigned boring busywork. Instead, we hope students are engaged in collaborative and productive tasks, especially the kind that deepen their learning, while the teachers meet with small groups to address need. In some cases, small group instruction does not allow for breakthrough results, and more intensive interventions are needed. Often, these interventions are provided by experts outside of the classroom, but classroom teachers can be involved in intensive interventions as well. The logistics of RTI can be complex, but the key message in this approach is that all students can learn if we are willing to examine our impact and adjust the learning environment accordingly.

Learning From What Doesn't Work

Thus far, we have focused our attention on influences that can positively impact students' learning. We explored surface, deep, and transfer levels of learning and noted that there are some things that work better at each level. We also discussed the ways in which teachers can determine their impact on student learning, and then respond when the impact is not as expected. Now, it's time to focus on some things that really don't work to build students' social studies learning. We don't want teachers to undo all of their hard work by engaging in practices that are harmful or that waste valuable learning time. Unfortunately, these are all too common in use. Even worse, many of these practices are the result of not focusing on one's impact, and instead spending time cataloging a student's shortcomings.

Grade-Level Retention

Students are often retained in a grade level based on their literacy achievement. The meta-analyses of this indicate that the practice is actually having the reverse effect, with an effect size of −0.32. As Frey (2005) and others have noted, grade-level retention for literacy achievement is not a defensible practice. Furthermore, we know that content-rich social studies instruction builds essential background knowledge essential for critical literacy skills. But schools and districts still hold onto the hope that another year of schooling will ensure that students learn to read and write at higher levels. Why would another year of the same curriculum, often using the same type of teaching and the same assessment tasks, make a difference? What most students who struggle need is not more of the same, but demonstrably different and better instruction, and teachers would be wise to consider RTI (e.g., Fisher & Frey, 2010), which has an effect size of 1.07. In most RTI efforts, students receive supplemental and intensive interventions throughout the year, delivered by knowledgeable adults who can monitor and adjust as needed to reach a desired level of achievement.

Ability Grouping

Another lesson educators should learn focuses on ability grouping. Simply said, there is no evidence to suggest that this practice will yield breakthrough results. The effect size of ability grouping is 0.30, negligible in terms of impact yet common in many schools. Some people argue that ability grouping works for advanced students, even if it doesn't work for struggling learners. The problem is it's not true. The effect of ability grouping is to disrupt the learning community, socially ostracize some learners, and compromise social skills, to name a few (Sapon-Shevin, 1994). And the effect on minority groups is much more serious, with more minority students likely to be in lower-ability classes destined to demonstrate to low performance often with the least effective teachers (Jimerson, 2001).

We have lost count of the number of times we have talked with well-meaning educators who hope that the solution to their students' achievement lies in grouping students by their perceived ability. Taking a grade level of students and giving one teacher the lowest-performing students, another teacher the average-performing students, and yet another, the highest-performing students may be popular, but the evidence is clear that it is not the answer. The two most common forms of ability grouping are

- Within-class grouping—putting students into groups based on the results of an assessment

- Between-class grouping—separating students into different classes, courses, or course sequences (curricular tracks) based on their previous academic achievement

The risk in writing this is that some readers will overgeneralize. Within-class and between-class ability grouping should be avoided. But needs-based instruction, with flexible groups, should not be eliminated. Student-centered teaching, basing instructional actions on students' understanding and then engaging students in small group learning, can be very effective. In fact, small group learning has an effect size of 0.49—provided the grouping is flexible, not fixed. The key to this approach is the condition that the groups change, and the instruction must match the needs of the learner. Let's look at the difference, occurring at the same school. In one sixth-grade classroom, the teacher administered a historical argument writing assessment and grouped her students based on their scores. The students with the lowest scores were in one group, slightly better writers formed a second group, and so on. She then met with groups over several weeks, providing instruction to each group. Sounds familiar and logical, right? It just didn't work. The post-assessments were no different from the original samples. The lowest-performing writers were still the lowest, but their scores inched up a barely perceptible amount. That was a lot of work for very little benefit.

Down the hall, another sixth-grade teacher administered the same historical argument writing assessment. She then analyzed the patterns of error found in her students' writing and continually regrouped students daily based on the error patterning. On one day, she met with a group of students who needed support with introductions and then with another group of students who needed guidance on supporting paragraphs. On another day, she focused her small-group instruction on students who needed help with their rebuttal paragraph and on another group of students who needed help with writing conclusions. In the same amount of time as was available to her colleague, she was able to address many of the instructional needs of her students using small groups. And the results speak for themselves. The average score increased a full performance level, and there wasn't a single student left in the lowest band on the rubric.

This teacher knows her impact because she calculates it herself. These may seem like subtle differences, but they are important. Small-group instruction is effective, but not when the intervention for the students is the ability of the group. The groups have to be flexible so that the instruction each group receives aligns with the students' performance and understanding.

Matching Learning Styles With Instruction

EFFECT SIZE FOR MATCHING STYLE OF LEARNING = 0.32

Another practice that has become widespread, but for which there is no supporting evidence, is matching learning styles with instruction. It may very well be that there are differences in how we prefer to access and share information, and that preference may change in different situations with different groups of people, but teaching students based on our perception of their particular type of intelligence is of very limited value. In fact, the effect size is 0.32. We know a student—we'll call him Joseph. He loves sports. He has played soccer since early childhood and basketball since elementary school, and consistently makes it to the all-star teams. He excels at every new sport that he tries. Some might say that he is gifted in the area of athletics. Others might say that his preferred learning style is active movement or callisthenic. Does that mean he is excused from developing historical thinking skills? Should we excuse his errors in analyzing primary sources? Should his teachers be encouraged to bring balls or sports' analogies into every single lesson? And if he's in class with students who have other preferences, should we separate him? No. Matching instruction with a perception of a learning style is not going to radically raise academic achievement. Why condemn Joseph to one form of learning (via movement), when indeed he may need to be taught other ways to learn? Let's acknowledge that there are differences in learners, but let's not label students (and not labeling students is really effective, with an effect size of 0.61). Instead, let's focus on instructional routines and habits that will ensure all students learn at high levels. Teachers may need to use multiple methods to capitalize on multiple ways of learning, but the mistake is to categorize students into one or more learning styles.

Test Prep

Test prep, including teaching test-taking skills, is another area for which there is insufficient evidence to warrant continued use. The effect size is 0.30, which translates to roughly half a year of achievement. We've all done it because there is an appeal to one's surface logic to teaching students generic test-taking skills. It just wastes a lot of precious time. Instead, teach learning and test-taking skills as an integral part of every lesson (not as a separate subject)—focus on teaching students the content and how to learn this content—as this has been shown to be much more effective in increasing student achievement on external measures of success. That's not to say that students shouldn't understand the format of the test, but that only takes a short time. They should also be taught about how to best prioritize time doing any task, as this can be a critical test-prep skill—but again do this within the context of the regular lessons—not some stand-alone skill. Test prep and teaching test-taking skills are consuming significant numbers of instructional minutes, despite the fact that we know there is no evidence that these accountability measures are going to inherently improve instruction or learning (Hattie, 2014). We are currently stuck with these types of tests, and students will likely face a wide range of tests over their lives (college admissions, food handling, and driving, to name a few). Studying content, and how to learn this content, especially using effective study skills techniques (with an effect size of 0.63), will pay much better dividends than trying to figure out how to beat the test.

> EFFECT SIZE FOR TEACHING TEST TAKING AND COACHING = 0.30

Homework

EFFECT SIZE FOR
HOMEWORK = 0.29

The final lesson we offer with respect to learning from what doesn't work, despite the fact that there are others, focuses on homework. Overall, homework has little impact on students' learning, with an effect size of 0.29. In this case, it's worth it to examine the value of homework at different grade levels. At the elementary level, homework has a limited impact on student learning, with an effect size of 0.10, whereas at the high school level, the effect size is 0.55. The major reason for these differences comes from the nature of homework. Homework that provides another chance to practice something already taught and for which a student has the beginnings of mastery can be effective (and much high school homework is of this nature), but homework that involves new materials, projects, or work with which a student may struggle when alone is least effective (and too much elementary homework is of this nature). Importantly, homework may not be the answer to students' achievement, and efforts to raise the rigor of schooling by assigning more independent learning that students complete at home are misguided and potentially harmful. Students can succeed just as much from what they do in school. Do not ask them to create a school at home where many students need adult expertise; while nearly all parents want to help their students, some do not know how.

Many parents can be poor teachers of schoolwork!

Thus far, we have focused on actions that do not work. We could have also focused on the finger-pointing common in some schools. Yes, mobility has a negative impact on students' learning, as does summer vacation. Hattie (2012) noted that about 50 percent of the achievement variation found in schools is attributed to student characteristics and demographics. Unfortunately, in many schools, that 50 percent gets all the play. After the students themselves, teachers have the biggest impact on student achievement, followed by school effects, the principal, parents, and the home. This is really, really important: a significant amount of the variance in student achievement is attributed to teachers. What teachers do matters. How teachers think really matters.

Making informed decisions about what actions to take, based on evidence, should be the focus of professional development sessions and grade-level or department conversations rather than admiring problems and blaming students for the conditions in which they live.

Conclusion

Measuring one's impact on student learning means that assessment is a prominent feature of the classroom. The purpose is not to grade the students' work, but to measure progress and compare it to the teaching that has occurred. Daily formative assessment is a chief way for teachers to make instructional decisions about what will occur next. Ways to check for understanding include asking questions, using exit tickets, and giving students lots of opportunities to self-assess. But these remain moment-in-time snapshots if not further contextualized through the administration and analysis of pre- and post-assessments and regularly paced progress monitoring. The assessments discussed in this chapter are a reminder of the many ways we have of tracking student progress. But it's what we do with them that counts. If assessment is used for nothing more than sorting students, we will continue to achieve the results we have always gotten. These assessments are measures of our progress, too—but only if we choose to look closely at our impact.

The risk to our students in failing to examine our impact is significant and damaging. The reliance on ineffective practices, such as in-grade retention and ability grouping, is the result of decisions by well-meaning but misguided adults who have focused their attention on the characteristics of students at the exclusion of the effectiveness of the instruction they have received. We should know our students well, and teach to their strengths while closely monitoring learning gaps. But the evidence is clear. Although what the student brings to school in terms of his or her learning background is important, a significant percentage of achievement variance lies within the teacher's influence (Hattie, 2009). Yet too often the vigor with which teachers locate explanations that lie with the student far outstrips their efforts to examine their impact on student learning and adjust accordingly.

This book has been about empowering educators to do exactly that. The profession is filled with dedicated people who have devoted their professional careers to improving the intellectual lives of children. Social studies education matters for the health of our democracies. And the good news is that teachers matter. We mean this not as coffee-cup sentimentality, but rather as an empowering sentiment. What teachers do matters when they scale learning to move from surface, to deep, to transfer of learning, and match approaches to their students' conceptual levels of knowledge. What teachers do matters when they monitor their impact and use that information to inform instruction and intervention. What teachers do matters when they reject institutional practices that harm learning. And best of all, what teachers do matters when they make social studies learning visible to their students, so students can become their own teachers.

VISIBLE LEARNINGplus® 250+ Influences on Student Achievement

To view a complete, updated list of the VISIBLE LEARNING® Influences and their effect sizes, please scan the QR Code below.

References

Almasi, J. F. (1994). The nature of fourth graders' sociocognitive conflicts in peer-led and teacher-led discussions of literature. *Reading Research Quarterly, 3*(3), 314–351.

Anderson, L. W., & Krathwohl, D. R. (2001). *A taxonomy for learning, teaching, and assessing: A revision of Bloom's taxonomy of educational objectives* (Abridged edition, 1st ed.). New York, NY: Person Education, Inc.

Anderson, R. C., Wilson, P. T., & Fielding, L. G. (1988). Growth in reading and how children spend their time outside school. *Reading Research Quarterly, 23*, 285–303.

Baker, S., Simmons, D., & Kame'enui, E. (1998). *Vocabulary acquisition: Synthesis of the research*. Washington, DC: US Department of Education, Office of Educational Research and Improvement, Educational Resources Information Center.

Berkeley, S., Marshak, L., Mastropieri, M. A., & Scruggs, T. E. (2011). Improving student comprehension of social studies text: A self-questioning strategy for inclusive middle school classes. *Remedial & Special Education, 32*(2), 105–113.

Biemiller, A. (2005). Size and sequence in vocabulary development: Implications for choosing words for primary grade vocabulary instruction. In E. H. Hiebert & M. L. Kamil (Eds.), *Teaching and learning vocabulary: Bringing research to practice* (pp. 223–242). Mahwah, NJ: Erlbaum.

Biggs, J. (1999). *Teaching for quality learning at university*. Buckingham, UK: Society for Research Into Higher Education and Open University Press.

Bransford, J. D., Brown, A. L., & Cocking, R. R. (Eds.). (2000). *How people learn: Brain, mind, experience, and school*. Committee on Developments in the Science of Learning and Committee on Learning Research and Educational Practice. Washington, DC: National Academy Press.

Brookhart, S. M. (2008). *How to give effective feedback to your students*. Alexandria, VA: ASCD.

Bruner, J.S. (1977). *The process of education* (2nd ed). Cambridge, MA: Harvard University Press.

Burek, D., & Losos, C. (2014). Debate: Where speaking and listening come first. *Voices From the Middle, 22*(1), 49–57.

Cazden, C. B. (1988). *Classroom discourse: The language of teaching and learning*. Portsmouth, NH: Heinemann.

Chesky, J., & Hiebert, E. H. (1987). The effects of prior knowledge and audience on high school students' writing. *Journal of Educational Research, 80*, 304–313.

Civic Online Reasoning Classroom Poster. (n.d.). Retrieved from https://sheg
.stanford.edu/civic-online-reasoning/classroom-poster

Coates, T. (June 2014). The case for reparations. *The Atlantic*. Retrieved from:
https://www.theatlantic.com/magazine/archive/2014/06/the-case-for
-reparations/361631/

Collins, J. (2001). *Good to great: Why some companies make the leap . . . And others
don't*. New York, NY: HarperBusiness.

Cronbach, L. J. (1942). An analysis of techniques for systematic vocabulary
testing. *Journal of Educational Research, 36*, 206–217.

Daywalt, D. (2013). *The day the crayons quit*. New York, NY: Philomel Books.

Deno, S. (1987). Curriculum-based measurement: An introduction. *Teaching
Exceptional Children, 20*, 41.

Doing Good Together™. (n.d.). Retrieved August 1, 2019, from https://www
.doinggoodtogether.org/

Donald, B. (2016, December 15). Stanford researchers find students have trouble
judging the credibility of information online. Retrieved July 18, 2019, from
https://ed.stanford.edu/news/stanford-researchers-find-students-have-trouble
-judging-credibility-information-online

Donovan, S., & Bransford, J. (2005). *How students learn*. Washington, DC: National
Academies Press.

Dweck, C. S. (2006). *Mindset: The new psychology of success*. New York, NY: Random
House.

Ellison, R. (1952). *Invisible man*. New York, NY: Random House.

Ferguson, L. E., Bråten, I. I., & Strømsø, H. I. (2012). Epistemic cognition when
students read multiple documents containing conflicting scientific evidence:
A think-aloud study. *Learning & Instruction, 22*(2), 103–120.

Fisher, D., & Frey, N. (2009). *Background knowledge: The missing piece of the comprehension puzzle*. Portsmouth, NH: Heinemann.

Fisher, D., & Frey, N. (2010). *Enhancing RTI: How to ensure success with effective
classroom instruction and intervention*. Alexandria, VA: ASCD.

Fisher, D., & Frey, N. (2012). Close reading in elementary school. *The Reading
Teacher, 66*(3), 179–188.

Fisher, D., & Frey, N. (2014). Close reading as an intervention for struggling
middle school readers. *Journal of Adolescent and Adult Literacy, 57*(5), 367–376.

Fisher, D., Frey, N., & Gonzalez, A. (2010). *Literacy 2.0: Reading and writing in the
21st century*. Bloomington, IN: Solution Tree.

Fisher, D., Frey, N., Anderson, H., & Thayre, M. (2015). *Text-dependent questions:
Pathways to close and critical reading, grades 6–12*. Thousand Oaks, CA: Corwin.

Flanagan, S., & Bouck, E. C. (2015). Mapping out the details: Supporting struggling writers' written expression with concept mapping. *Preventing School
Failure, 59*(4), 244–252.

Flavell, J. (1979). Metacognition and cognitive monitoring: A new area of cognitive-
developmental inquiry. *American Psychologist, 34*, 906–911.

Follett, K. (2010). *Fall of giants: The century trilogy, Book 1*. New York, NY: Dutton.

Follett, K. (2012). *Winter of the world: Century trilogy, Book 2*. New York, NY: Dutton.

Follett, K. (2014). *Edge of eternity - Book 3 - Century*. London, UK: Pan Macmillan.

Frey, N. (2005). Retention, social promotion, and academic redshirting: What do
we know and need to know? *Remedial and Special Education, 26*(6), 332–346.

Frey, N., & Fisher, D. (2010, November). Modeling expert thinking. *Principal Leadership. 11*(3), 58–59.

Frey, N., & Fisher, D. (2013). *Rigorous reading: Five access points for helping students comprehend complex texts, K–12*. Thousand Oaks, CA: Corwin.

Goddard, R. D., Hoy, W. K., & Hoy, A. W. (2000). Collective teacher efficacy: Its meaning, measure, and impact on student achievement. *American Educational Research Journal, 37*, 479–507.

Graham, S., & Perin, D. (2007). *Writing next: Effective strategies to improve writing of adolescents in middle and high schools*. New York, NY: Carnegie Corporation of New York.

Graves, M. F. (1986). Vocabulary learning and instruction. *Review of Educational Research, 13*, 49–89.

Graves, M. F. (2006). *The vocabulary book: Learning and instruction*. New York, NY: Teachers College.

Guthrie, J., & Klauda, S. (2014). Effects of classroom practices on reading comprehension, engagement, and motivations for adolescents. *Reading Research Quarterly, 49*(4), 387–416.

Guthrie, J. T., & Wigfield, A. (2000). Engagement and motivation in reading. In M. L. Kamil, P. B. Mosenthal, P. D. Pearson, & R. Barr (Eds.), *Handbook of reading research* (Vol. III, pp. 403–424). Mahwah, NJ: Erlbaum.

Hattie, J. (n.d.). *Visible Learning, that make the difference in education* [PowerPoint presentation]. Visible Learning Laboratories, University of Auckland, New Zealand. Retrieved from http://docplayer.net/4137828-Visible-learning-that -make-the-difference-in-education-john-hattie-visible-learning-labora tories-university-of-auckland.html

Hattie, J. (2009). *Visible learning: A synthesis of over 800 meta-analyses relating to achievement*. New York, NY: Routledge.

Hattie, J. (2012). *Visible learning for teachers: Maximizing impact on learning*. New York, NY: Routledge.

Hattie, J. (2014). The role of learning strategies in today's classrooms. 34th Vernon Wall Lecture. Retrieved from https://shop.bps.org.uk/publications/34th -vernon-wall-lecture-2014-john-a-c-hattie.html

Hattie, J., & Yates, G. (2014). *Visible learning and the science of how we learn*. Oxson, UK: Routledge.

Henderson, L. L., Weighall, A., & Gaskell, G. (2013). Learning new vocabulary during childhood: Effects of semantic training on lexical consolidation and integration. *Journal of Experimental Child Psychology, 116*(3), 572–592.

Hess, D. E., & McAvoy, P. (2014). *The political classroom: Evidence and ethics in democratic education*. New York, NY: Routledge.

Hoy, W. K., Sweetland, S. R., & Smith, P. A. (2002). Toward an organizational model of achievement in high schools: The significance of collective efficacy. *Educational Administration Quarterly, 38*(1), 77–93.

Hyland, K., & Hyland, F. (Eds.). (2006). *Feedback in second language writing: Contexts and issues*. Cambridge, MA: Cambridge University Press.

Jerald, C. D. (2007). *Believing and achieving (Issue brief)*. Washington, DC: Center for Comprehensive School Reform and Improvement.

Jimerson, S. R. (2001). Meta-analysis of grade retention research: Implications for practice in the 21st century. *School Psychology Review, 30*(3), 420–437.

Johnson, P., & Keier, D. (2011). *Catching readers before they fall*. York, ME: Stenhouse.

Kahneman, D. (2011). *Thinking fast, thinking slow*. New York, NY: Farrar, Straus & Giroux.

Kuhn, D. (2000). Metacognitive development. *Current Directions in Psychological Science, 9*(5), 178–181.

Larson, B. (1999). Influences on social studies teachers use of classroom discussion. *The Social Studies, 90*(3), 125–132. Retrieved June 09, 2019, from https://www.jstor.org/stable/30189533?seq=1#page_scan_tab_contents

Levine, P., & Kawashima-Ginsberg, K. (2017, September 21). The Republic is (still) at risk—and civics is part of the solution. A briefing paper for the Democracy at a Crossroads National Summit. Retrieved from https://www.civxnow.org/static/media/SummitWhitePaper.fc2a3bb5.pdf

Linnenbrink, E. A., & Pintrich, P. R. (2003). The role of self-efficacy beliefs in student engagement and learning in the classroom. *Reading & Writing Quarterly: Overcoming Learning Difficulties, 19*, 119–137.

Loewen, J. W., Stefoff, R., & Loewen, J. W. (2019). *Lies my teacher told me: Everything American history textbooks get wrong*. New York, NY: The New Press.

Lublin, J. (2003). *Deep, surface and strategic approaches to learning*. Dublin, IRL: University College Dublin Centre for Teaching and Learning.

Marton, F., & Säljö, R. (1976, February). On qualitative differences in learning: 1—Outcome and process. *British Journal of Educational Psychology, 46*(1), 4–11.

Marzano, R. J., & Pickering, D. J. (2005). *Building academic vocabulary: Teacher's manual*. Alexandria, VA: ASCD.

Mathisen, G. E., & Bronnick, K. S. (2009). Creative self-efficacy: An intervention study. *International Journal of Educational Research, 48*, 21–29.

McNamara, D. S., & Kintsch, W. (1996). Learning from texts: Effects of prior knowledge and text coherence. *Discourse Processes, 22*, 247–282.

Mehta, J., & Fine, S. M. (2019). *In search of deeper learning: The quest to remake the American high school*. Cambridge, MA: Harvard University Press.

Michaels, S., O'Connor, M. C., Hall, M. W., & Resnick, L. B. (2010). *Accountable Talk® sourcebook: For classroom conversation that works* (v. 3.1). Pittsburgh, PA: University of Pittsburgh Institute for Learning. Retrieved from http://ifl.lrdc.pitt.edu

Monte-Sano, C., Paz, S. D., & Felton, M. (2014). *Reading, thinking, and writing about history: Teaching argument writing to diverse learners in the common core classroom, grades 6-12*. New York, NY: Teachers College Press.

Moore, D. W., & Readence, J. E. (1984). A quantitative and qualitative review of graphic organizer research. *Journal of Educational Research, 71*(1), 11–17.

Murphy, P. K., & Alexander, P. A. (2002). What counts? The predictive powers of subject-matter knowledge, strategic processing, and interest in domain-specific performance. *Journal of Experimental Education, 70*(3), 197–214.

Murphy, P. K., Wilkinson, I. A. G., Soter, A. O., Hennessey, M. N., & Alexander, J. F. (2009). Examining the effects of classroom discussion on students' comprehension of text: A meta-analysis. *Journal of Educational Psychology, 101*(3), 740–764.

Nagy, W. E. (1988). *Teaching vocabulary to improve reading comprehension*. Urbana, IL: National Council of Teachers of English.

National Council for the Social Studies (NCSS). (2013). *The college, career, and civic life (C3) framework for social studies state standards: Guiding for enhancing the rigor of K-12 civics, economics, geography, and history*. Silver Spring, MD: NCSS.

Ngozi Adiche, C. (2013). *Americanah*. New York, NY: Alfred Knopf.

Nystrand, M. (2006). Research on the role of classroom discourse as it affects reading comprehension. *Research in the Teaching of English, 40*, 392–412.

Palincsar, A. S. (2013). Reciprocal teaching. In J. Hattie & E. Anderman (Eds.), *International guide to student achievement* (pp. 369–371). New York, NY: Routledge.

Palincsar, A. S., & Brown, A. (1984). Reciprocal teaching of comprehension-fostering and comprehension-monitoring activities. *Cognition and Instruction, 1*(2), 117–175.

Paris, S. G., Lipson, M., & Wixson, K. (1983). Becoming a strategic reader. *Contemporary Educational Psychology, 8*, 293–316.

Pauk, W., & Owens, R. J. Q. (2010). *How to study in college* (10th ed.). Boston, MA: Wadsworth/Cengage Learning.

Paul, R. & Elder, L. (2013). *How to write a paragraph: The art of substantive writing* (3rd ed.). Tomales, CA: Foundation for Critical Thinking.

Perkins, D. N., & Salomon, G. (1992). Transfer of learning. *International encyclopedia of education* (2nd ed.). Oxford, UK: Pergamon.

Priebe, S., Keenan, J., & Miller, A. (2012). How prior knowledge affects word identification and comprehension. *Reading & Writing, 25*(1), 131–149.

Protheroe, N. (2008, May). Teacher efficacy: What is it and does it matter? *Principal*, 42–45.

Richards, R. I. (1929). *Practical criticism: A study of literary judgment*. London, UK: Routledge & Kegan Paul.

Robertson, J., Riley, M., & Willis, A. (2016, March). How to hack an election. *Bloomberg Businessweek*. Retrieved from https://www.bloomberg.com/features/2016-how-to-hack-an-election/

Rockman, S. (2005). Liberty is land and slaves: The great contradiction. *OAH Magazine of History, 19*(3), 8–11. doi:10.1093/maghis/19.3.8

Rubie-Davies, C. M. (2015). *High and low expectation teachers: The importance of the teacher factor*. New York, NY: Psychology Press.

Sapon-Shevin, M. (1994). *Playing favorites: Gifted education and the disruption of community*. Albany, NY: State University of New York Press.

Scarry, R. (2015). *What do people do all day?* New York, NY: HarperCollins.

Shuster, K. (2018, January 31). Teaching hard history. Retrieved June 27, 2019, from https://www.splcenter.org/20180131/teaching-hard-history

Shuster, K., & Meany, J. (2005). *Speak out! Debate and public speaking in the middle grades*. New York, NY: International Debate Education Association.

Smith, I. (2007). *Sharing learning intentions*. London, UK: Learning Unlimited.

Smith, T. W., Baker, W. K., Hattie, J. A. C., & Bond, L. (2008). A validity study of the certification system of the National Board of Professional Teaching Standards. In L. Ingvarson & J. A. C. Hattie (Eds.), *Assessing teachers for professional certification: The first decade of the National Board of Professional*

Teaching Standards (pp. 345–380). Advances in Program Evaluation Series #11. Oxford, UK: Elsevier.

Stahl, S. A., & Fairbanks, M. M. (1986). The effects of vocabulary instruction: A model-based meta-analysis. *Review of Educational Research, 56*(1), 72–110.

Stanovich, K. E. (1999). *Who is rational? Studies of individual differences in reasoning.* Mahwah, NJ: Erlbaum.

Stern, J., Ferraro, K., & Mohnkern, J. (2017). *Tools for teaching conceptual understanding, secondary.* Thousand Oaks, CA: Corwin.

Stricht, T. G., & James, J. H. (1984). Listening and reading. In P. D. Pearson, R. Barr, M. L. Kamil, & P. Mosenthal (Eds.), *Handbook of reading research* (Vol. 1, pp. 293–317). White Plains, NY: Longman.

Swanson, E. (June 2, 2014). Americans can't even stomach an apology for slavery, much less reparations. *Huffington Post.* Retrieved from https://www.huffpost .com/entry/reparations-poll_n_5432116

Swanson, E., Hairrell, A., Kent, S., Ciullo, S., Wanzek, J. A., & Vaughn, S. (2014). A synthesis and meta-analysis of reading interventions using social studies content for students with learning disabilities. *Journal of Learning Disabilities, 47*(2), 178–195.

Tierney, R. J., Readance, J., & Dishner, E. (1995). *Reading strategies and practices: A compendium* (4th ed.). Boston, MA: Allyn & Bacon.

Tomlinson, C. A. (2005). *How to differentiate instruction in mixed-ability classrooms.* Alexandria, VA: ASCD.

We Need Diverse Books. (2019, July 31). Retrieved August 1, 2019, from https:// diversebooks.org/

Wiggins, G. (1989). The futility of trying to teach everything of importance. *Educational Leadership, 47*(3), 44–59.

Wiggins, G. (1998). *Educative assessment: Designing assessments to inform and improve student performance.* San Francisco, CA: Jossey-Bass.

Wilkinson, I. A. G., & Nelson, K. (2013). Role of discussion in reading comprehension. In J. Hattie & E. Anderman (Eds.), *International guide to student achievement* (pp. 299–302). New York, NY: Routledge.

Wineburg, S. S. (1991). On the reading of historical texts: Notes on the breach between school and academy. *American Educational Research Journal, 28*(3), 495–519. https://doi.org/10.3102/00028312028003495

Wineburg, S. (2018). *Why learn history (when it's on your phone).* Chicago, IL: University of Chicago Press.

Wineburg, S. (2019, February 12). The internet is sowing mass confusion. *USA Today.* Retrieved June 27, 2019, from https://www.usatoday.com/story/ opinion/2019/02/12/internet-confusion-rethink-education-digital-sputnik -moment-column/2769781002/

Winograd, P. N. (1984). Strategic difficulties in summarizing texts. *Reading Research Quarterly, 19*, 404–425.

Wood, T. (1998). Alternative patterns of communication in mathematics classes: funneling or focusing? In H. Steinbring, M. G. Bartolini Bussi, & A. Sierpinska (Eds.), *Language and communication in the mathematics classroom* (pp. 167–78). Reston, VA: National Council of Teachers of Mathematics.

Index

All students should have the opportunity to be successful!

Visible Learning^{plus}™ is based on one simple belief: Every student should experience at least one year's growth over the course of one school year. Visible Learning^{plus}™ translates the groundbreaking Visible Learning research by professor John Hattie into a practical model of inquiry and evaluation. Bring Visible Learning to your daily classroom practice with these additional resources across mathematics, literacy, science, and social studies.

Imagine students who understand their educational goals and can monitor their own progress. This illuminating book focuses on self-assessment as a springboard for markedly higher levels of student achievement.

Nancy Frey, John Hattie, and Douglas Fisher

Written for elementary and secondary educators, this is a must-have road map for implementing concept-based teaching.

Julie Stern, Nathalie Lauriault, Krista Ferraro, and Juliet Mohnkern

Easy to follow templates and tools guide educators to use learning intentions and success criteria and align standards seamlessly. Students achieve because learning is purposeful and expectations are clear.

Douglas Fisher, Nancy Frey, Olivia Amador, and Joseph Assof

Learn how you can implement Hattie's ten mindframes to maximize student success and become a better teacher or leader.

John Hattie, Klaus Zierer, and Raymond L. Smith

To order, visit corwin.com

TMN20333

A SAGE Publishing Company

Helping educators make the greatest impact

CORWIN HAS ONE MISSION: to enhance education through intentional professional learning.

We build long-term relationships with our authors, educators, clients, and associations who partner with us to develop and continuously improve the best evidence-based practices that establish and support lifelong learning.